The Hockey News

Transcontinental Books
5800 Saint-Denis Street
Suite 900
Montreal, Que. H2S 3L5
Tel.: 514-273-1066
Toll-free: 1-800-565-5531
www.tcmedialivres.com

**Bibliothèque et Archives nationales du Québec and Library and
Archives Canada cataloguing in publication**

Main entry under title :
The big book of hockey fun
At head of title : The hockey news.
ISBN 978-1-92763-209-3
1. Hockey players - Biography. I. Shuker, Ronnie.
II. Hockey news (Montréal, Québec). III. Title.
GV848.5.A1B53 2014   796.962092'2   C2014-941938-4

Art Direction & Design: Erika Vanderveer
Player Caricatures: Robert Ullman

Project Editor: Ronnie Shuker
Fact-checker: Casey Ippolito
Copy Editor: Curtis Ng
Proofreader: Luke Sawczak

Cover Photo Credits:
Drew Doughty & Jonathan Toews: Bill Smith/NHLI via Getty Images
Sidney Crosby: Gregory Shamus/NHLI via Getty Images
Jonathan Bernier: Graig Abel/NHLI via Getty Images

Printed in Canada
© Transcontinental Books, 2014
Legal deposit – 4th Quarter 2014
National Library of Quebec
National Library of Canada

We acknowledge the financial support of the Government
of Canada through the Canada Book Fund.

THE BIGBOOK BOOK HOCKEY OF FUN!

EDITED BY

RONNIE SHUKER

Transcontinental Books

DEDICATED

TO

HOLTER & **HEATH**

CONTENTS

INTRODUCTION

LAST SPRING, SHELLY ANDERSON, THN'S trusty Pittsburgh correspondent, asked the Penguins for an interview with Sidney Crosby to write a story about him in *The Big Book of Hockey Fun!* The Pens told her they'd forward her request to Crosby, but that a 1-on-1 interview was highly unlikely. He was restricting media access so that he could focus all his attention on the playoffs, which was understandable. After all, Crosby has been hunting for a second Stanley Cup since winning his first in 2009, and he wanted to put all his energy into preparing for the post-season.

All that changed, however, once Crosby found out the interview was for a kids' book. And so in the middle of a playoff run, the most sought after player on the planet sat down for a face-to-face chat with Anderson, which turned into the player profile for our Pittsburgh Penguins chapter (pg. 140).

That's the kind of heart hockey players have when it comes to kids. NHLers live a charmed life, no doubt: playing in packed stadiums, flying in first-class jets, sleeping in five-star hotels, schmoozing with celebrities and cashing fat paychecks. But it's a real-life adult existence that all started with a dream as a kid, and players remember the days when they, too, were fantasizing about one day playing in the NHL.

To make those dreams come true, however, required huge amounts of discipline and hard work. In his interview, Crosby opened up about the sacrifices he had to make as a kid if he wanted to get to the NHL: working a newspaper route (a job he hated) to earn money for hockey, practising his skills after school instead of hanging out with friends and going to bed early the night before a game instead of stay-

ing out late to party. The hardest sacrifice, though, was resisting his mom's mouthwatering, melt-in-your-mouth chocolate chip cookies (his favorite) so that he'd stay in peak physical condition.

The pages that follow are filled with stories like Crosby's. In them, we profile 30 NHL stars, one on every team. But there's more. So much more. Players share their memories of their first NHL game and list off their favorite things, so if you want to know what Crosby eats for his pre-game meal or what video game he plays during his down time (spoiler alert: spaghetti with meat sauce and *GoldenEye*), then we've got you covered. As a bonus, we've put your puzzle solving skills to the test with a word search and crossword of your favorite team.

The fun starts with the Anaheim Ducks and Ryan Getzlaf, whose NHL dream as a kid began on the frozen ponds near Regina, Sask. **- RONNIE SHUKER**

RYAN GETZLAF

KIDS LIKE TO PLAY VIDEO GAMES AND WATCH television. As a boy, Ryan Getzlaf was like any other kid in that regard, but he wasn't very good at gaming and wasn't too interested in what was on the tube. *Hockey Night in Canada* was must-see TV Saturday nights but not necessarily for him.

Growing up in a residential part of Regina, Sask., Ryan and the other kids on the block were about enjoying the outdoors. Warm summers were spent on the streets. Cold winters, sometimes brutal ones on the flatlands, were spent there, too. Or on icy ponds.

"We had a street there where anywhere from 10 to 20 kids all grew up in the same age group," Ryan said. "We played a lot of sports. We all grew up playing baseball, football, hockey – everything like that. When we grew up, we didn't know any better. We played street hockey in the winter, and it didn't matter what the temperature was."

Sports were big in the Getzlaf household, with Ryan and his older brother Chris competing on various teams. The two are just a couple years apart, and Ryan often tagged along with his sibling, whether Chris liked it or not.

"We had our years where we had battles and he didn't want me around," Ryan said. "Obviously, being the kid brother, I was always wanting to be with him and his friends. I remember a couple of times, he'd chase me around the block, and I'd do the same to him. As high school started, that's when I really started being friends with him and his friends. And now we have the same group of friends that we basically grew up with from high school on."

The two found their own paths. Chris stayed with football and is a seven-year veteran slotback in the Canadian Football League. He won his first Grey Cup with the Saskatchewan Roughriders in 2013.

Ryan is the accomplished leader of the Anaheim Ducks.

Ryan's success came earlier in his career, reaching the top of the NHL in his sophomore season, when Anaheim won the Stanley Cup in 2007. Since then, Ryan has also won two Olympic gold medals with Team Canada. He's always had the natural talent. It just took years of hard work to take it to the highest level.

Ryan played four seasons with the Calgary Hitmen of the Western League, where he was one of the team's top players. The Ducks had two first-rounders in the 2003 draft, and they used them to set the franchise up for years to come. They took Ryan 19th overall then grabbed Corey Perry nine picks later.

> ## WE ALL PLAYED STREET HOCKEY IN THE WINTER, AND IT DIDN'T MATTER WHAT THE TEMPERATURE WAS

15
RYAN
GETZLAF
BORN: MAY 10, 1985
HEIGHT: 6' 4"
WEIGHT: 221 lbs
POSITION: C
SHOOTS: R

The two are now right up there with the NHL's other top duos, including Pittsburgh's Sidney Crosby and Evgeni Malkin and Chicago's Jonathan Toews and Patrick Kane. The pair came up as talented freshmen with Anaheim in 2005-06 and blossomed as sophomores on its 2006-07 championship team. And they've fed off each other for nine seasons. Ryan's playmaking helped Perry win the Hart Trophy in 2011, and Perry's ability to finish plays and score helped Ryan become a finalist for it in 2014.

When you think of the Ducks, you think of Getzlaf and Perry. That's what Ryan wanted when he signed an eight-year contract extension in 2013 and helped convince Perry to do the same. Ryan's father, Steve, served as a sounding board at the time. The bond between father and son is as tight as ever, with the two often talking on the telephone and dad occasionally visiting his hockey-playing son in southern California or other NHL stops.

"He's got a good head on his shoulders," Steve said. "He knew what he wanted, and he knew where he wanted to stay. He always discusses things with me, which is nice. I like to be a part of it."

The road to stardom hasn't always been smooth. In 2011-12, Ryan slumped to a career-low 11 goals, and his 57 points were his fewest since his rookie season. The pressures of being the captain on a struggling club and being a first-time father affected his play. But just two seasons later, after finding a better balance between his professional and personal life, Ryan was back to being an elite NHLer.

"There's always going to be different times in your life where things are a little more heated and tougher to go through," said Ryan, who has three children with his wife, Paige. "Right now, everything is where we want it to be and where my wife and I envisioned ourselves at this point." – **ERIC STEPHENS**

MY FAVORITE...

Movie: *Wedding Crashers*

Actor: *Owen Wilson*

Musician: *Tim McGraw*

Pre-game meal: *Pasta, chicken, prosciutto and mozzarella cheese*

Food: *Steak*

Restaurant: *Mastro's Ocean Club in Newport Beach*

NHL city: *Anaheim*

NHL arena: *Scotiabank Saddledome. I like playing in Calgary because it's almost like my second home*

Vacation spot: *Fiji*

Car: *Ferrari 458 Italia*

Sport other than hockey: *Football*

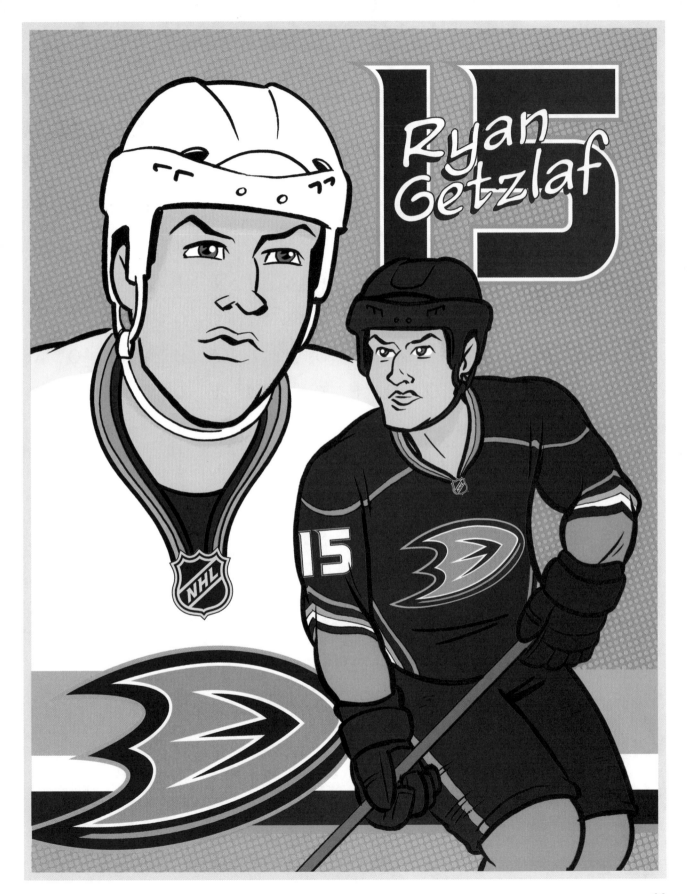

WORD SEARCH

BOB MURRAY
MIGHTY
COREY PERRY
PACIFIC
PAUL KARIYA
CARLYLE
STANLEY CUP
GETZLAF
SELANNE
STONER
HONDA
WILD WING
BOUDREAU
RYAN KESLER

B	R	E	L	S	E	K	N	A	Y	R	O	B
O	R	E	T	U	S	N	A	Z	R	S	P	X
U	C	B	O	B	M	U	R	R	A	Y	E	G
D	F	K	P	A	C	I	F	I	C	C	H	N
R	A	I	S	L	E	F	G	Q	E	O	I	I
E	L	R	S	O	Y	M	A	H	N	R	O	W
A	Z	O	E	E	S	J	P	D	T	E	R	D
U	T	P	A	U	L	K	A	R	I	Y	A	L
B	E	L	Y	L	R	A	C	I	U	P	T	I
L	G	G	Q	E	M	H	N	Z	G	E	D	W
E	I	R	E	N	O	T	S	N	H	R	Y	E
R	N	E	S	I	J	A	P	H	E	R	Z	Y
S	T	A	N	L	E	Y	C	U	P	Y	D	K

→ My First
GAME

October 5, 2005
Anaheim Ducks 5
@ Chicago Blackhawks 3
1 shot, 10:16 ice time

RYAN
GETZLAF

"The day was nerve-wracking. I got up and did my morning skate. I don't think I slept too much that afternoon. It was a different experience getting ready for the game and going to the rink. I got on the bus and saw everybody there, my teammates. It's a pretty exciting time. Walking to the locker room and having some of the guys that were around our room at the time, I remember looking at all their stalls and then mine was up there too."

CROSSWORD

ACROSS

1 Anaheim's team was once known as the ___ Ducks
3 Another Anaheim-based sports franchise
7 Bryan ___, pictured, wears the number 55
8 A ___ player like No. 11 Down has plenty of nifty moves
9 The logo of No. 3 Across has an 'A' topped by a ___
11 Many ex-NHLers have ___ playing in the league (like the Sutters, for example)
14 Scores
16 No. 17 Across was born under this zodiac sign
17 Paul ___ was Ducks captain
18 Ryan Getzlaf's hometown

DOWN

1 Bob ___ is Ducks GM
2 Both coach Bruce Boudreau and center Andrew Cogliano hail from this city, which also has NHL hockey
4 ___ Etem is a first-round pick of the Ducks from 2010
5 Hampus Lindholm is from here
6 Boudreau was a Maple ___ in his playing days
10 Corey Perry was named to the NHL's first ___-___ team in 2011
11 Teemu ___ holds team records for just about everything
12 The Ducks had a 13-game home winning ___ in 2012-13
13 Getzlaf and Perry represented ___ at the Sochi Games
15 ___ Koivu was an alternate captain in Anaheim

Mascot
"Wild Wing"

AHL Affiliate
Norfolk Admirals

ECHL Affiliate
Utah Grizzlies

FAST FACTS

Captain: ***Ryan Getzlaf***
Coach: ***Bruce Boudreau***
GM: ***Bob Murray***
Arena: ***Honda Center***
Capacity: ***17,174***
Stanley Cups: ***1***
Playoff Appearances: ***10***
First Season: ***1993-94***

SHANE DOAN

SHANE DOAN HAD AN IMMEDIATE FONDNESS for the Arizona desert, with its towering cacti and sunsets that blushed overhead. It was the setting of his favorite film, *Tombstone*, a classic Western sifting right from wrong. That slight familiarity with the Valley of the Sun was enough to intrigue Shane when the franchise that drafted him seventh overall in 1995, the Winnipeg Jets, relocated to Phoenix the following year and became the Coyotes.

And the 98-degree Fahrenheit change in temperature from the morning he left Winnipeg to the afternoon he stepped off the plane in Phoenix certainly pleased him. But it was something else that kept him there through a six-season playoff drought, bankruptcy court and the subsequent four-year search for ownership. And that was loyalty.

"I do really appreciate that for four years of seven, four, five and six goals they still kept me around," Shane said. "I really, really appreciated that, because my NHL career could have been over."

Adversity tends to stick in the memory longer than accolades, and that's why Shane can recite his goal output from his first four NHL seasons – because they weren't up to snuff, in his mind. Maybe they weren't, but there was plenty to be proud of by reaching the pros from Halkirk, Alta., population 121.

"When I made it to Kamloops to play junior hockey, it was a big deal," Shane said. "And then when I got drafted, that was a big deal. When I got to play in the NHL, that was a big deal."

But just being there wasn't enough. Shane wanted to perform and become a mainstay and, above all else, win. So a demotion to the American League in 1997-98 didn't sit well with him. He took the assignment, though, and eventually rebounded. Two seasons later, he surpassed 25 goals and 50 points and has kept humming along at nearly that pace ever since.

In 2003, he was named captain of the Phoenix Coyotes, who changed their name to the Arizona Coyotes in 2014. He's regularly represented Canada in international play, winning gold at the 2004 World Cup and participating in the 2006 Winter Olympics. All of this increased his profile, which defined him as one of the game's premier power forwards with a passion that's unique even among hockey players.

"The day he came in, he was just a big happy kid," said Stan Wilson, the Coyotes' head equipment manager, who's become Shane's confidant. "He hasn't changed a whole lot in that part, to be honest. That's what's amazing."

> THE DAY HE CAME IN, SHANE WAS JUST A BIG HAPPY KID. HE HASN'T CHANGED A LOT. THAT'S WHAT'S AMAZING

Shane became eligible for free agency in 2007, but he bypassed it, instead signing a five-year extension with the Coyotes. During the length of this contract, the franchise was thrust into bankruptcy and teetered on the brink of yet another relocation while the NHL searched for a new ownership group.

In the midst of this uncertainty, Shane's contract expired, and he was again able to explore free agency. Unlike the previous time, he entertained offers but eventually chose to remain with the franchise.

"They had choices all along, and they'd stuck by me and given me the benefit of the doubt when probably other teams might not have," Shane said. "My first four years in the league, I wasn't very good. They stuck by me. When someone probably would have given up on me, they gave me opportunity."

But Shane's decision wasn't solely based on loyalty to the organization. All four of his children have been raised in Arizona, and he and his wife, Andrea, have established a home there. In 2013, the Coyotes finally secured an ownership group whose intent was to keep the franchise right where it is.

Amid all this turmoil, it seemed fitting for the team to have a leader who weathered his own challenges when it would've been easier to move on. It's only fair, then, that Shane has become synonymous with the Coyotes. Usually, that type of recognition is planted on a league superstar, a title Shane humbly shrugs off. And perhaps rightfully so. His point totals won't rank among the elite in the record books, but packaged with his persona as a tireless worker, loyal leader and fierce competitor, he's set an example of how to achieve a meaningful career. To some, that just might be more valuable.

"By no means am I satisfied," Shane said. "But my career has been a dream come true."

– SARAH MCLELLAN

MY FAVORITE...

Movie: *Tombstone*

TV show: *Knight Rider*

Celebrity: *Viggo Mortensen*

Band: *Needtobreathe*

Player growing up: *Paul Coffey*

Team growing up: *Edmonton Oilers*

Pre-game meal: *On the road, it's the usual: spaghetti and chicken parmigiana. At home, I try to have eggs, toast and potatoes*

Junk food: *Ice cream*

Video game: *Whatever my sons are playing*

Sport other than hockey: *I love all sports. I don't know if I could pick one*

Hockey memory: *Winning the World Cup in 2004 is pretty amazing. To be associated with it in any way was pretty awesome*

Way to score: *One-timer*

WORD SEARCH

YANDLE
JETS
ROENICK
TKACHUK
BOEDKER
MIKE SMITH
SHANE DOAN
GRETZKY
VITALE
HOWLER
DUBNYK
TIPPETT
WINNIPEG
GLENDALE

D	Q	R	W	I	N	N	I	P	E	G	F	K
R	D	I	J	R	R	A	N	O	E	L	S	U
S	H	A	N	E	D	O	A	N	R	T	A	H
H	O	H	G	K	T	Y	Q	N	T	A	N	C
T	W	A	R	D	L	S	O	E	A	E	L	A
I	L	M	E	E	T	A	P	Y	L	B	O	K
M	E	D	T	O	G	P	R	A	W	M	K	T
S	R	S	Z	B	I	P	T	N	W	J	Y	V
E	O	L	K	T	U	I	H	D	L	E	N	A
K	N	U	Y	T	V	H	C	L	B	C	B	W
I	A	N	H	K	C	I	N	E	O	R	U	A
M	G	L	E	N	D	A	L	E	K	T	D	N
I	H	L	H	N	A	Q	K	I	S	T	S	S

→ *My First*
GAME

October 7, 1995
Dallas Stars **5**
@ Winnipeg Jets **7**
2 A, 2 shots, 2 PIM

SHANE
DOAN

"I was playing with Alexei Zhamnov and Igor Korolev. I was so excited, obviously, to play in the NHL. I had a couple assists because those guys were so good. Igor had an unbelievable start to the year. Jason Doig, Craig Mills and I were all 18 years old or under 20, which I think hadn't been done after that until Colorado did it a few years ago. It was one of those things I'll never forget. I didn't score for a really long time. It took me 17 games to score – big surprise – after that, but I remember that first game very clearly."

CROSSWORD

ACROSS

1 Former Coyote Radim ___ is from the Czech Republic
3 Keith ___, pictured, is an alternate captain
7 ___ Doan wears the 'C'
8 Oliver Ekman-___ was born in Sweden
9 The 2002 Winter Olympics were held in nearby ___ Lake City
11 Advance the puck up the ice
14 Ex-Coyotes coach Wayne Gretzky won the ___ ___ Trophy 10 times
16 Former netminder Sean ___ is the goalie coach in Phoenix
17 Thomas ___ backed up starter Mike Smith in 2013-14
18 Derek ___ is from Edmonton, where Gretzky once starred

DOWN

1 Disappear
2 Dave ___ is behind the bench in Arizona
4 Suits up
5 Finish
6 Left winger ___ Bissonnette
10 ___ Vermette plays center for Arizona
11 Mike ___ had his contract bought out by the team in 2014
12 Getting ready to play, ___ up
13 Martin Hanzal played his junior hockey for the Red Deer ___
15 The Coyotes once shared their building with this NBA team

Mascot
"Howler the Coyote"

AHL Affiliate
Portland Pirates

ECHL Affiliate
Gwinnett Gladiators

FAST FACTS

Captain: **Shane Doan**

Coach: **Dave Tippett**

GM: **Don Maloney**

Arena: **Jobing.com Arena**

Capacity: **17,125**

Stanley Cups: **0**

Playoff Appearances: **19**

First Season: **1979-80**

MILAN LUCIC

MILAN LUCIC MADE IT TO THE NHL WHEN HE was 19 years old, without ever having played a minor league game. Just four years before that, however, there were people in the hockey world who thought he might not even play at the major junior level in the Western League, never mind professionally.

It just shows what determination, motivation, belief in oneself and a love for the game can do. Milan has already played seven years in the NHL, been to the playoffs every season and helped the Boston Bruins win a Stanley Cup in 2011. He's considered one of the league's best power forwards – a big, strong left winger who loves to play a physical game, but also has the skill to score 30 goals. And to think that when he wasn't selected in the 2003 WHL bantam draft, Milan wondered for a little while if he still wanted to play the sport he'd loved since he first put on skates at the age of four.

"To go through that experience at 15 years old – a young age – it was the first time I had to deal with any adversity when it came to hockey," Milan said. "Someone basically telling you you're not good enough was a tough thing to overcome. But after having some time to think, I knew I still loved the game of hockey. I knew there was still an opportunity to move up and try to make it to the NHL."

> ## SOMEONE BASICALLY TELLING YOU YOU'RE NOT GOOD ENOUGH WAS A TOUGH THING TO OVERCOME

Hockey had always been fun for Milan, who grew up in Vancouver and had an uncle, Dan Kesa, who played for the NHL's Canucks. But all sports were fun for Milan. He played basketball, rugby, baseball and lacrosse, though it wasn't hard for him to choose which sport to continue playing.

"I loved hockey more than anything," he said. "I enjoyed it the most."

Getting left out of the bantam draft hurt. He believed he was as good as many of the players who got drafted, and it frustrated him to hear that some people didn't think he skated well enough to play at higher levels.

But he didn't want to stop playing and give up his dream of reaching the NHL. Milan played one more minor hockey season as a midget and then started trying out for teams at lower junior levels. He played briefly for the Jr. B Delta Ice Hawks, but coach Sean Crowther of the Coquitlam Express, a coach in the Jr. A British Columbia League, had noticed Milan and added him to the team.

While playing for the Express, Milan caught the eye of Scott Bonner, general manager of his hometown WHL team, the Vancouver Giants. By the end of the season, Bonner had added Milan to the roster. It was a big moment for Milan, and for the Giants.

After his first season in the WHL, Milan was picked by the Bruins in the second round (50th overall) of the 2006 draft because they liked his hard-hitting game and thought he'd develop into a good scorer. The Bruins were right. In Milan's second season with Vancouver, he scored 30 goals during the regular season and was named MVP of the Memorial Cup, which the Giants won in that 2006-07 season.

Milan was named captain of the Giants for 2007-08, but he never got the chance to wear the 'C' on

IT WAS MY LOVE OF THE GAME THAT HELPED ME OVERCOME WHAT ANYONE TRIED TO SAY ABOUT ME

his jersey. He impressed first-year coach Claude Julien so much in training camp that the Bruins kept him on the team. By the playoffs, Milan was playing on the top line with Marc Savard and Glen Murray.

Milan has gone on to become a favorite of Bruins fans, who love tough hockey and appreciate it even more when hard-hitting players contribute in other ways. He's come a long way since 2003, when he decided it was up to him to prove people wrong about his potential.

"My love of the game and my competitiveness motivated me," Milan said. "It was my love of the game and having so much fun playing the game that helped me overcome what anyone tried to say about me." **– MIKE LOFTUS**

MY FAVORITE...

Movie: *Casino*

Band: *Metallica*

Celebrity: *Leonardo DiCaprio*

Video game: *Sonic the Hedgehog*

Pre-game meal: *Pasta*

Junk food: *Oreos*

Player growing up: *Jarome Iginla*

Sport other than hockey:

To watch: *Tennis*   To play: *Basketball*

Hockey memory: *Winning the Stanley Cup in my hometown of Vancouver*

Way to score: *Any way*

WORD SEARCH

KREJCI
ZDENO CHARA
CHIARELLI
CAM NEELY
SHORE
CHERRY
BOURQUE
JULIEN
MARCHAND
ESPOSITO
ORR
RASK
GARDEN
BERGERON

```
C  S  G  A  R  D  E  N  A  B  O  W  S
K  N  I  S  G  G  O  H  I  O  T  H  A
M  A  R  C  H  A  N  D  Z  U  O  M  I
N  L  T  Q  A  O  O  Z  D  R  R  V  L
E  O  T  I  S  O  P  S  E  Q  R  D  L
C  P  I  R  B  E  A  U  N  U  U  B  E
A  Y  C  S  E  C  N  U  O  E  S  V  R
M  Y  J  Y  R  R  E  H  C  U  R  R  A
N  E  E  Y  G  S  I  N  H  L  A  N  I
E  T  R  S  E  D  L  R  A  S  K  C  H
E  B  K  I  R  P  U  Z  R  S  N  O  C
L  Q  X  K  O  L  J  O  A  N  C  N  P
Y  A  N  E  N  A  X  L  S  S  E  M  Q
```

My First
GAME

October 5, 2007
*Boston Bruins **1***
*@ Dallas Stars **4***
1 shot, 5 PIM, 6:53 ice time

MILAN
LUCIC

"Of all the games I've gone into, even Game 7 of the Stanley Cup final, the first game of my NHL career was the most nervous I've ever been. To be lucky enough to play as a 19-year-old, there were obviously a lot of nerves. My parents flew to Dallas for that first game. In warmups, I was looking over at Mike Modano. That was really cool, seeing a guy I grew up watching. I got into a fight in the second period. It was one of those things to do to prove myself. We lost, but the game is a memory I'll always cherish."

CROSSWORD

ACROSS

1 David ___ had another big season for the Bruins
3 Goaltender ___ Rask, pictured
7 Defeated narrowly
8 Milan Lucic is one of No. 1 Across' ___
9 Bobby Orr was the first defenseman to win the Art ___ Trophy
11 Something for Rask to hug
14 Bruins great ___ Bourque
16 Boston took Dougie Hamilton ninth overall in the 2011 ___
17 When Orr was the Bruins' top scorer, teammate Phil Esposito was in ___ place
18 Jarome ___ played one season (2013-14) in Boston

DOWN

1 Former Bruin Steve ___ was known as 'The Friendly Ghost'
2 Coach Julien, and namesakes
4 Penalty ___ like Chris Kelly get a lot of ice time when Boston is shorthanded
5 Help in the scoring of a goal, like No. 1 Across often does
6 Faceoff (or a tie game)
10 Zdeno Chara captained the Slovakian team at the ___ Games in Sochi
11 Goalies like Rask wear lots of ___ to prevent injuries
12 Team that joined the NHL way back in 1924
13 Chara's team before coming to Boston as a free agent
15 Coaches don't like players who take ___ penalties

Mascot
"Blades the Bruin"

AHL Affiliate
Providence Bruins

ECHL Affiliate
South Carolina Stingrays

FAST FACTS

Captain: *Zdeno Chara*

Coach: *Claude Julien*

GM: *Peter Chiarelli*

Arena: *TD Garden*

Capacity: *17,565*

Stanley Cups: *6*

Playoff Appearances: *69*

First Season: *1924-25*

MATT ZAMBONIN/FREESTYLE PHOTO/GETTY IMAGES

25

CODY HODGSON

WHEN CODY HODGSON WAS A KID, EVERYTHING was about hockey. He played it, he wrote about players for homework, and he and his brother Clayton watched games to study how to get better. Cody wrote in his journal that he wanted to be in the NHL when he grew up. He always thought he could make it. It seemed pretty easy, actually. While growing up in Haliburton, Ont., he was surrounded by guys who had played in the league.

Glen Sharpley, who played for the Minnesota North Stars and Chicago Blackhawks, sharpened Cody's skates at the local sports store. Cody's favorite restaurant was owned by Walt McKechnie, who played in nearly 1,000 games. Cody worked out in a gym run by Ron Stackhouse, who played defense for the Pittsburgh Penguins and Detroit Red Wings. His friend Phil was the son of former NHL enforcer Basil McRae.

> THE NHL WASN'T A FAR-OFF DREAM BECAUSE THERE WERE SO MANY GUYS THAT PLAYED IN THE NHL AROUND ME

"Playing in the NHL was never something that was a far-off dream because there were so many guys that played in the NHL around me," Cody said. "I was always asking these guys questions. They always said, 'It can be done.' "

Cody knew he was close to his dream in 2008, when he was the 10th player picked in the NHL draft. The Vancouver Canucks chose him after he scored 40 goals for his Ontario League team, the Brampton Battalion. After the draft, he had another great year, with 43 goals and 92 points in 53 games. The OHL named him player of the year, and he was voted most sportsmanlike player, too. Brampton made it all the way to the league championship. Things were going great.

Then, during the summer of 2009, Cody hurt his back. It was bad. Very bad. He couldn't skate. He was a sturdy 19-year-old, yet he couldn't lift things anymore. The doctors told him he had a bulging disc, which tore the outer layer between two of his vertebrae, causing the soft inner layer to painfully protrude. They said he'd feel better soon, but they were wrong on both accounts.

Cody didn't get well quickly. He was hurt for a whole year. No one knew why his back didn't get better. He played in only 24 of Brampton's 79 games. When he went to Vancouver for the playoffs, the doctors said he couldn't play. He was still too injured. Cody started to think he'd never get better.

"Being hurt is a brutal thing, especially not knowing why you are hurt," he said. "Once you know what it is, you can fix it and get better. It's just not knowing if it's ever going to get better and not knowing if you're going to be able to play again that's tough."

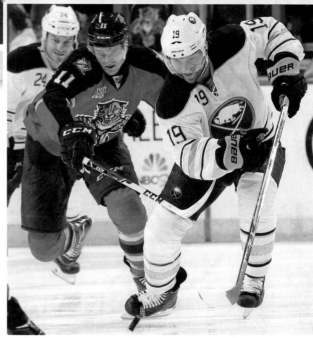

In the summer of 2010, someone finally helped. Cody worked out with Gary Roberts, an ex-NHLer who'd played in the league 21 years, the final 11 of which came after Roberts' career almost ended because of a neck injury.

"Just watching him move in the gym, I said, 'Cody, something's not right,' " Roberts said.

Roberts and his doctors found that an important muscle in Cody's back was torn. They treated it and Cody was back to normal.

"It was an amazing feeling waking up in the morning with no pain," Cody said.

Cody was again ready to make it to the NHL. He soon did, but he learned an important lesson along the way: there will be bumps in the road.

Cody's hard work continues every summer. He still trains with Roberts. They run, lift weights, work on their balance, eat healthy foods and get the right amount of sleep. The extra effort allowed Cody to lead the Buffalo Sabres in points and power play goals in 2013-14.

Cody always wanted to score goals in the NHL, but he's discovered something else even more fun: hanging out with his teammates. The talks in the dressing room are a blast. He loves learning about players' families. For road games, he likes travelling with the guys and seeing new cities.

"Getting to know your teammates is the most fun for me," Cody said. "I still keep in contact with players from Brampton, even the guys that aren't in the National Hockey League. It's the memories that you make along the way that make it special."

Cody makes sure other people enjoy the games, especially those who are hurt. He brings sick or injured Canadian police officers to Buffalo and gives them tickets. They also get a tour of the dressing room and meet the Sabres.

MY FAVORITE...

Movie: *Happy Gilmore*

TV Show: *How I Met Your Mother*

Celebrity: *Angelina Jolie*

Musician: *Michael Bublé*

Video game: *NHL 2004*

Pre-game meal: *Brown rice, chicken, pasta sauce, salad*

Junk food: *Ice cream*

Player growing up: *Steve Yzerman*

Team growing up: *Detroit Red Wings*

Sport other than hockey: *Beach volleyball*

Hockey memory: *Winning the world juniors in Canada in 2009*

Way to score: *Deke*

Meeting players as a kid is what showed Cody he could make it to the NHL. He thought it would be fun. And he was right.

"We're fortunate to live the lives we live," he said. "It's nice to be able to do it as an adult." – JOHN VOGL

WORD SEARCH

THE AUD
LAFONTAINE
TIM MURRAY
PERREAULT
CONNECTION
NOLAN
RUFF
ENROTH
HODGSON
NIAGARA
PYSYK
IMLACH
ENNIS
SABRETOOTH

S	S	N	I	A	G	A	R	A	C	O	W	F
A	N	O	S	G	D	O	H	I	S	T	O	L
B	C	I	H	T	O	R	N	E	I	I	M	A
R	L	T	Q	A	O	O	Z	M	G	M	V	F
E	R	C	L	N	E	P	L	Y	I	M	D	O
T	P	E	R	R	E	A	U	L	T	U	B	N
O	Y	N	S	V	C	N	U	O	D	R	V	T
O	Y	N	P	H	L	K	F	F	U	R	L	A
T	E	O	Y	R	S	S	N	O	L	A	N	I
H	T	C	S	Z	E	D	I	O	A	Y	C	N
F	B	V	Y	D	P	E	Z	N	S	N	O	E
Y	Q	X	K	Q	L	U	O	I	N	C	N	P
T	H	E	A	U	D	X	L	S	S	E	M	Q

My First
GAME

February 1, 2011
Vancouver Canucks **4**
@ Dallas Stars **1**
2 shots, 9:52 ice time

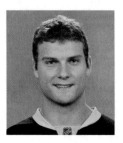

CODY
HODGSON

"I just came off a shattered orbital bone, so I still had a full cage on. The guys hid my helmet before warmup. They said, 'You can't go out for warmup in your first NHL game with a mask on.' There was an ice storm, so there were only 4,000 people in the stands. When you walk to the rink from the hotel, there's a big hill there, and the hill was just covered in ice. We slid down the hill in our suits.

"The NHL gives you the game sheet, and my name was scratched off because they made an error in my name."

CROSSWORD

ACROSS

1 Jhonas ___, pictured, is in net
3 The Sabres are best known for the '___ Connection' line, which featured Gilbert Perreault
7 Ted ___ is again behind the bench in Buffalo
8 Birthplace of No. 11 Down
9 Former Sabres broadcaster Harry Neale once coached the ___ State Buckeyes
11 Skirmish
14 To badly beat a defender is to ___ him
16 Former Sabre Ville ___ had his contract bought out in 2014
17 ___ Tallinder is an alternate captain
18 Another of the teams in Buffalo's division

DOWN

1 Finish
2 Hometown of No. 10 Down (it's also an Atlantic Division city)
4 Buffalo plays at First ___ Center
5 The Sabres have retired No. 2, worn by Tim ___ (now better known for his coffee shops)
6 Spear
10 Cody ___ is among the team's top scorers
11 Marcus ___'s father, Mike, also played for the Sabres
12 Penalize
13 Scotty ___ was both coach and GM in Buffalo
15 Dominik Hasek ___ out Sabres opponents 13 times in 1997-98 to earn the Hart Trophy as league MVP

Mascot
"Sabretooth"

AHL Affiliate
Rochester Americans

ECHL Affiliate
Elmira Jackals

FAST FACTS

Captain: **Vacant**

Coach: **Ted Nolan**

GM: **Tim Murray**

Arena: **First Niagara Center**

Capacity: **19,070**

Stanley Cups: **0**

Playoff Appearances: **29**

First Season: **1970-71**

MARK GIORDANO

REACHING THE TOP THROUGH HARD WORK AND determination – Mark Giordano understands that journey.

Mark went from being an undrafted addition who believed he was destined for university instead of the professional ranks to captain of the Calgary Flames. He's motivated to bring success to his team, which is in the middle of a rebuild.

It's a tough position for a veteran player to accept – playing on a team building from the ground up as it attempts to acquire the talent (often young talent) needed to build a Stanley Cup-contending team – and many veterans opt for greener pastures. However, Mark responded with the best season of his career after being named captain just before the start of 2013-14.

"This is the organization that gave me a chance," Mark said. "There aren't too many guys who get the opportunity I got.... There's a lot of loyalty that goes into it from my end. This is a great organization, with great people around us as players. For them to name me captain, put that trust in me – I really wanted to prove them right."

Leadership and character are attributes all teams covet. It's even more important when a team is struggling in the standings and inserting young pros into the roster. Mark's ability to guide comes from experience.

At the conclusion of his junior career with the Ontario League's Owen Sound Attack, Mark figured his future was studying business at York University and had already enrolled in school before receiving an invitation to the Flames' summer prospect camp. When it ended, he was offered a contract.

> IT WAS A THREE-WAY DEAL, AND I WAS MAKING PRETTY MUCH THE MINIMUM IN ALL THREE LEAGUES

"It was a three-way contract," Mark said. "We had an East Coast Hockey League affiliate, and I was making pretty much the minimum in all three leagues. It was basically a take-it-or-leave-it thing.

"In the first year, I didn't think I'd even stick in the American League in a lockout year, because there were a lot of NHL players who were going to be on our team and we were a split team with Carolina. There weren't too many spots, but somehow I made it."

He was the leading scorer of the Flames' AHL affiliate in Omaha in 2005-06 and received the call for his NHL debut in January of that season, eventually playing seven games for the Flames. It was a few weeks before getting the summons that Mark finally believed he could play in the world's top league.

"I was having a pretty good year, and Richie Regehr got called up before me," Mark said. "Watching him play, and he was doing really well in the NHL, I figured if Richie could play well, I knew I could get a chance."

A deserved chance, it would seem.

"Clearly he flew under the radar for a long time, but when I was playing with him in the minors, I knew right away that he was going to be a heck of

MY FAVORITE...

TV show: *Breaking Bad*

Celebrity: *Roger Federer*

Band: *Nirvana*

Video game: *Madden*

Pre-game meal: *Two chicken breasts, rice, sweet potato and soup*

Junk food: *Nibs*

Player growing up: *Wendel Clark*

Team growing up: *Toronto Maple Leafs*

Sport other than hockey: *Baseball*

Hockey memory: *Scoring my first two NHL goals in Toronto in front of my family and friends. We were able to stay overnight after the game so I could visit with them*

Way to score: *One-timer from the slot, not from way back – a clean one-timer with no screen that I blow by the goalie. It's hard, but that's why it's my favorite*

a player," said former teammate Eric Nystrom. "He had the ability to take over games in the AHL. He was so strong, and his skill was really underrated. He's turned out to be a great player.

"He didn't just make it – he's the captain of an NHL team and one of the best players."

Mark spent the bulk of 2006-07 with the Flames, but afterward he made a bold decision. Instead of accepting a two-way contract, which would have made it easier for him to be sent to the minors, he went to play for Moscow Dynamo in Russia, thinking he'd remain a bubble player in the NHL.

After his hiatus, he was offered a one-way contract with Calgary and worked from being a regular in the lineup to becoming the team's best player.

Mark relishes that his story can make him a role model for young players.

"It's great for kids who may be having a tougher time to realize you don't have to be the superstar to make it," he said. "There's a lot of room for guys who work hard and play the right way." – **RANDY SPORTAK**

WORD SEARCH

HARTLEY
MACINNIS
IGINLA
ATLANTA
MONAHAN
HARVEY
SADDLEDOME
LANNY
STANLEY CUP
HUDLER
GIORDANO
BRIAN BURKE
FLETCHER
KARRI RAMO

```
H  C  F  L  E  T  C  H  E  R  I  G  B
G  I  L  A  X  H  U  B  K  P  S  P  E
I  E  K  R  U  B  N  A  I  R  B  S  P
H  A  R  T  L  E  Y  G  P  B  A  I  L
S  I  E  I  K  E  I  H  Q  E  G  N  C
O  C  L  A  N  N  Y  X  U  E  I  N  V
S  A  D  D  L  E  D  O  M  E  O  I  O
N  T  U  A  U  S  D  L  O  A  R  C  D
M  L  H  V  A  U  V  Z  N  L  D  A  E
Z  A  Z  Q  Y  E  V  R  A  H  A  M  U
Y  N  M  H  E  S  R  I  H  N  N  Y  T
R  T  K  A  R  R  I  R  A  M  O  O  Y
I  A  P  U  C  Y  E  L  N  A  T  S  K
```

→ My First
GAME

January 30, 2006
Calgary Flames **2**
@ St. Louis Blues **3**
2 PIM, 14:01 ice time

MARK
GIORDANO

"In the minors on the weekends, we played Friday, Saturday and Sunday. I was told after the game to get to St. Louis on Monday for a game that night. It was four games in four nights for me, but I was so pumped to get the call I wasn't tired. Before the game, I was really nervous, and I remember sitting on the bench being in awe. Once I got the first couple shifts, the nerves started to go away. I played two games, went back to the minors and was called up again at the end of the season. It was a cool year for me."

CROSSWORD

ACROSS

1. Area reserved for Jonas Hiller and Karri Ramo
3. Brian, Darryl and Brent ___ all coached the Flames
7. When the NHL playoffs begin
8. 'Bearcat' Murray was a much-loved ___ in Calgary
9. ___ Suter was Calgary's first Calder Trophy winner
11. Player aged 9-10
14. Used a certain joint illegally
16. Flames legend Lanny McDonald began his NHL career with the Maple ___
17. He's at center in Calgary
18. ___ Iginla was known as 'Iggy' while wearing the 'C'

DOWN

1. The Flames used to play at Stampede ___
2. Calgary won its only ___ Cup in 1989
4. Where captain Mark Giordano hails from
5. Coach Hartley's full first name
6. Given name of No. 17 Across
10. When the Flames and Oilers meet, it's 'The Battle of ___'
11. Where the Flames were based before coming to Calgary
12. Calgary's ___ Wideman, pictured
13. Aim
15. ___ King was coach in Calgary back in the 1990s

Mascot
"Harvey the Hound"

AHL Affiliate
Adironack Flames

ECHL Affiliate
Colorado Eagles

FAST FACTS

Captain: **Mark Giordano**

Coach: **Bob Hartley**

GM: **Brad Treliving**

Arena: **Scotiabank Saddledome**

Capacity: **19,289**

Stanley Cups: **1**

Playoff Appearances: **26**

First Season: **1972-73**

JEFF SKINNER

JEFF SKINNER IS VERY COMFORTABLE IN HIS skates, and he should be. Coming from a family in which all six children were figure skaters, Jeff was one of the best figure skaters in his age group for Ontario.

The Skinner kids – two boys and four girls – also had some pretty good hockey players in their ranks. Jeff's older brother Ben even shared a dressing room with Jeff when both were members of the Ontario League's Kitchener Rangers for a season. But Jeff's preternatural skill on blades was obvious from the start.

"The first time he was on skates he was probably two and a half," said Jeff's father, Andrew Skinner. "He was striding right away. It was as if he had a low center of gravity. He could go end to end."

Jeff took up figure skating at six years old and continued until he turned 13. He was one of the top-ranked skaters in Ontario, winning a bronze medal at the 2004 Skate Canada Junior Nationals, but a bruised growth plate steered his attention to hockey full time. Doctors told Jeff he had to stay away from practising figure skating jumps because of the stress double axels or triple jumps would put on his body.

"He was off his figure skates and told to avoid

> THE FIRST TIME JEFF WAS ON SKATES HE WAS PROBABLY TWO AND A HALF. HE WAS STRIDING RIGHT AWAY

jumps for 10 weeks," Andrew said. "That was a turning point. Once he had that break from competition, it was hard to get back into it."

There was no such problem in hockey, however, as Jeff continued his ascent through the minor ranks. He was always one of the best players for his age, even if he wasn't the biggest kid. He also had some pretty big inspirations in his older twin sisters who played collegiate hockey – Jennifer at Harvard and Andrea at Cornell.

"They were great role models for me growing up," Jeff said. "I remember going to their games and seeing how cool it was to play in front of those crowds. It left a good impression. The success they had was inspiring for me, seeing their work ethic and where it got them."

He was soon on a similar trajectory. Following in the footsteps of his brother, Jeff came to Kitchener for 2008-09. The Rangers were in rebuild mode, but Jeff still showed tremendous promise by putting up 27 goals and 51 points in 63 games.

He stayed with the same billet family as his brother, and his parents made the trek over from Markham, Ont., for Friday night home games (a one-way trip is about an hour and 20 minutes), easing the transition.

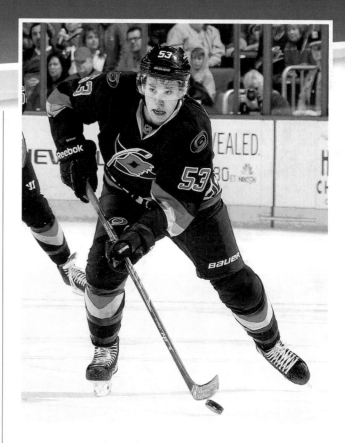

The next season, Ben went on to Wilfred Laurier University in nearby Waterloo, but it was Jeff who took everyone to school. In a breakout performance, he rang up 50 goals and 90 points in 64 games before a stunning playoff run that featured 20 goals in 20 games. The timing was great. Jeff was up for the NHL draft in 2010 and had caught the eye of the Carolina Hurricanes, who ended up taking him seventh overall.

At the Hurricanes' summer rookie camp, Jeff impressed everyone with his strength on the ice, and by the time Carolina had to make the tough decisions in the fall, it was Jeff earning his NHL jersey ahead of several other prospects who'd been with the organization longer. What followed was the stuff of NHL dreams.

The Hurricanes began the season in Europe, playing their first two games in Helsinki, Finland, against the Minnesota Wild. Carolina took the first game. In the second, Jeff made his mark in another win. He got his first NHL point, assisting on a Tuomo Ruutu goal, then sealed the deal by winning the game in the shootout. The Skinner clan watched that game from home, and Jeff's ascension was really becoming clear.

"The game came back on from a commercial break, and the full TV screen was filled with Jeff's face as the first shooter in the shootout," Andrew said. "We all let out some sort of noise over that."

From there it was a magical campaign for Jeff. He had 15 points in his first 15 games and kept the offense going. He ended the season with 31 goals and 63 points, playing in all 82 games and leading all NHL rookies in points. He also decided three games via the shootout.

The cherry on top, of course, was the Calder Trophy for rookie of the year, an award a player can

MY FAVORITE...

Movie: *300*

Cartoon: *Mighty Morphin Power Rangers*

Video game: *EA Sports NHL series*

Junk food: *Ice cream*

Jersey: *Toronto Maple Leafs*

Memorabilia: *Pittsburgh Penguins jersey signed by Sidney Crosby*

only win once. Jeff faced stiff competition from San Jose's Logan Couture and Michael Grabner of the New York Islanders, but in the end there was no denying the kid in Carolina.

"On the ice, he's extraordinarily competitive and driven," Andrew said. "He tried to do the best he can in anything, whether it was sports or school."

For a kid who coveted his family's figure skating trophies as a boy, Jeff already has some pretty impressive hardware of his own. **- RYAN KENNEDY**

WORD SEARCH

BRINDAMOUR
STORMY
CAM WARD
FAULK
SEKERA
TLUSTY
ERIC STAAL
FRANCIS
HARTFORD
JORDAN
KHUDOBIN
RUTHERFORD
STANLEY CUP
RALEIGH

S	Q	K	H	U	D	O	B	I	N	E	O	B
R	E	L	Y	Q	G	H	B	K	P	S	B	E
U	C	K	R	R	H	G	I	E	L	A	R	A
T	R	F	E	D	A	L	C	P	B	A	I	L
H	L	L	L	R	E	J	O	R	D	A	N	C
E	A	E	K	O	A	A	F	U	E	I	D	F
R	A	Y	D	F	F	D	R	A	W	M	A	C
F	T	B	M	T	S	D	A	J	A	U	M	D
O	S	T	V	R	U	N	E	L	E	O	E
R	C	Z	Q	A	O	H	C	K	B	C	U	U
D	I	T	H	H	R	T	I	E	N	I	R	T
R	R	I	W	P	Y	T	S	U	L	T	T	Y
I	E	P	U	C	Y	E	L	N	A	T	S	K

My First GAME

October 7, 2010

Carolina Hurricanes **4**
@ Minnesota Wild **3**
2 shots, 16:26 ice time

JEFF
SKINNER

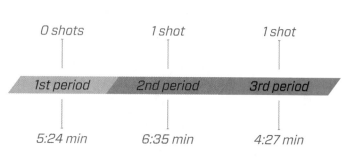

0 shots   1 shot   1 shot

1st period   2nd period   3rd period

5:24 min   6:35 min   4:27 min

CROSSWORD

ACROSS

1 Jiri ___ is a Czech-born Hurricane
3 Former goaltender Justin ___
7 Was in favor of; ___ for
8 Keith ___ was once captain in Carolina, succeeded by Ron Francis
9 Mark left by a healed cut (or the bad guy in *The Lion King*)
11 The Hurricanes had a franchise record 52 ___ in 2005-06
14 Ron Francis is the general ___
16 Unmarked
17 Widen
18 Defenseman Jay Harrison is from ___, Ont.

DOWN

1 Number worn by captain Eric Staal
2 The Staals hail from ___ Bay, Ont.
4 Carolina is in the NHL's ___ Conference
5 Puts a teammate in scoring position (two words)
6 Teams like the Hurricanes report to training ___ in mid-September
10 Riley Nash is from this Alberta town
11 The Hurricanes came from Hartford, where they were known by this nickname
12 Cam Ward won the Conn ___ Trophy in 2006
13 Andrej ___, pictured, is a Slovakian defenseman
15 ___ Ley was captain when the franchise was launched in Hartford in 1979

Mascot
"Stormy"

AHL Affiliate
Charlotte Checkers

ECHL Affiliate
Florida Everglades

FAST FACTS

Captain: *Eric Staal*

Coach: *Bill Peters*

GM: *Ron Francis*

Arena: *PNC Arena*

Capacity: *18,680*

Stanley Cups: *1*

Playoff Appearances: *13*

First Season: *1979-80*

JONATHAN TOEWS

JONATHAN TOEWS SHOWED PROMISE RIGHT from the start. His dad, Bryan Toews, remembers him walking through the house in his skates.

"He had been skating by the time he was three and a half and had a stride at four," Bryan said. "That blew my mind."

Jonathan first realized around 12 or 13 that he could really do something special in hockey. Soon afterward, that led him to one of several key decisions he made as a teenager. At 15, he decided to pull up stakes in Winnipeg and head down to Minnesota to attend Shattuck-St. Mary's, a prep school whose hockey program had already spun out Sidney Crosby, Zach Parise and Jack Johnson.

"At first, we said no way," Bryan said. "He was way too young."

But several factors worked in Shattuck's favor. By attending the school, Jonathan would not only get a great education and continue to play high-level hockey, he'd also be preserving his NCAA eligibility, which became important a few years later.

As with many of the kids who commit to Shattuck's, Jonathan had his most important stretch in the first six to eight weeks, when homesickness is at its worst. But the dorm room atmosphere and the fact that players live with their teammates seven days a week eventually turned the group into something close to a family. And just to make things a little more interesting, Jonathan combined three years of high school into two so he could get to the University of North Dakota sooner. He was a freshman at 17, playing on one of the best teams in the nation. Despite his age, Jonathan excelled as a rookie on the Fighting Sioux, finishing fourth in team scoring with 22 goals and 39 points in 42 games.

The three players who had more points than him – Drew Stafford, Travis Zajac and T.J. Oshie – are all impact players in the NHL now. They're each a couple years older.

> JONATHAN THOUGHT HE COULD DO IT. BUT WE THOUGHT, 'MAN, HE'S PLAYING AGAINST MEN IN THE NCAA'

"Jonathan thought he could do it," Bryan said. "But we thought, 'Man, he's playing against men there.'"

But being nearly a point-per-gamer at a top school will get a player noticed in a lot of corners, and Jonathan was no exception. Heading into the 2006 draft, his name was being bandied about as someone to watch near the top.

On draft day, the St. Louis Blues opted to take Erik Johnson, a big U.S. National Team Development Program defenseman, with the first selection. Although that wasn't much of a shock, there was uncertainty in pick No. 2, which belonged to the

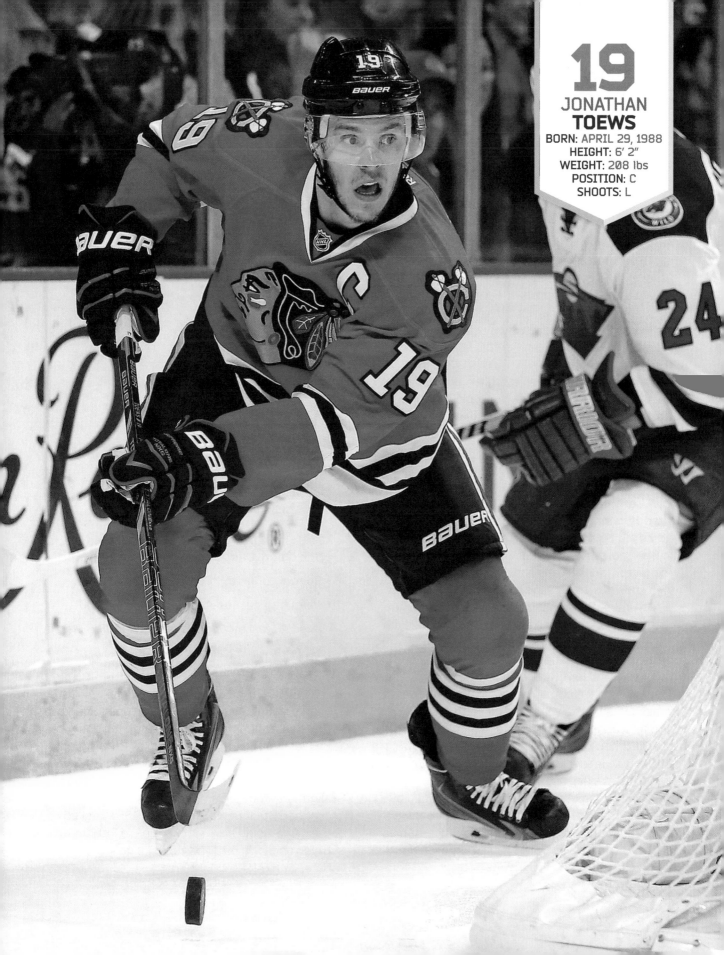

Pittsburgh Penguins. Jonathan thought he was going to become a Pen, but the honor went to Jordan Staal of the Peterborough Petes instead. That's when the nerves kicked in.

"I really thought when Pittsburgh took Staal that I might slide down to sixth or seventh," Jonathan said. "But going to Chicago third, I was the luckiest guy that day."

Which, at the time, seemed a little crazy. After all, despite having the second-overall pick, Pittsburgh was already armed with Sidney Crosby, Evgeni Malkin and Marc-Andre Fleury, while the Blackhawks had nothing. But the venerable franchise, a laughingstock at the time, wasn't far from better days.

Chicago made Patrick Kane its first pick overall in 2007, and he made the leap straight to the NHL that year. Jonathan joined him and the pair was locked at the hip from the beginning. With no expectations in Chicago, the two burgeoning stars were allowed to grow organically and had a coach in Denis Savard who knew what it was like to be an elite talent.

"He understood what it takes for a player to get comfortable," Jonathan said. "It's tough for a skill player not to get minutes when you're young."

Savard gave his charges that opportunity, and they rewarded him. Kane went on the win the Calder Trophy as rookie of the year, while Jonathan established himself as a young leader on the team.

In fact, Jonathan was such a respected player in the Blackhawks' room that he was named captain in 2008-09. He was just a sophomore at the time, and only 20 years old, but his ability to impact a team quickly became obvious. Savard was replaced by Joel Quenneville, and with defenders Duncan Keith and Brent Seabrook joining Kane and Jonathan as serious building blocks, the Hawks were suddenly a force to be reckoned with.

MY FAVORITE...

Movie: *The Pursuit of Happyness*

Cartoon: *Looney Tunes*

Musician: *Jason Aldean*

Video game: *Call of Duty*

Junk food: *Chocolate*

School subject: *French*

Memorabilia: *Los Angeles Kings Wayne Gretzky jersey (signed by players like Marty McSorley and Kelly Hrudey but not Gretzky)*

By 2009-10, no one could stop Chicago. The Hawks swept the top-seeded San Jose Sharks in the Western Conference final and then beat the Philadelphia Flyers for the Stanley Cup. Not only did Jonathan, as captain, become the first Hawk in 49 years to hoist the Cup, he also got closure on his slight draft day slide.

"When Staal won the Cup (in 2009), I asked Jonathan if he would have rather gone to Pittsburgh," Bryan said. "He said, 'Nope, we're going to win it here.'" – **RYAN KENNEDY**

WORD SEARCH

QUENNEVILLE
SAVARD
STAN MIKITA
HULL
BOWMAN
KEITH
TOEWS
CRAWFORD
SEABROOK
GLENN HALL
ESPOSITO
UNITED CENTER
PATRICK KANE
SHARP

S	H	K	H	U	D	K	B	I	N	E	R	B
P	Q	U	E	N	N	E	V	I	L	L	E	E
A	C	K	L	R	H	O	S	W	E	O	T	A
T	R	K	E	L	A	T	S	P	B	E	N	L
R	G	L	E	N	N	H	A	L	L	S	E	C
I	A	E	L	I	A	A	F	U	E	P	C	V
C	A	Y	U	R	T	D	R	A	W	O	D	C
K	T	B	P	T	N	H	A	J	A	S	E	S
K	W	T	S	T	A	N	M	I	K	I	T	A
A	C	D	Q	A	M	H	C	Z	B	T	I	V
N	D	R	O	F	W	A	R	C	N	O	N	A
E	R	I	K	O	O	R	B	A	E	S	U	R
I	E	S	J	A	B	R	L	O	K	T	S	D

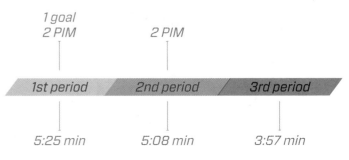

CROSSWORD

ACROSS

1 ___ Hossa is from Slovakia
3 Denis ___'s No. 18 has been retired in Chicago
7 Jonathan ___ wears the 'C'
8 Hossa played three seasons in this now defunct NHL city
9 Gets physical; ___ the body
11 ___ Muldoon put a famous curse on the Blackhawks
14 Coach Joel Quenneville hails from this Ontario border city, a recent Memorial Cup winner
16 Another number retired by the Hawks
17 Heckle
18 A forward or defenseman (but not a goalie)

DOWN

1 Stan ___ was a Blackhawk for 22 seasons
2 He still leads the team with 926 career ___
4 Corey Crawford allowed just 57 goals ___ in 30 games in 2012-13
5 Norris Trophy winner ___ Keith is a mainstay on the blueline
6 The crease is the goalie's ___
10 Where Doug Wilson, another Norris-winning Hawk, is now GM
11 ___ Sharp, pictured, is an alternate captain
12 Marcus Kruger's homeland
13 The Hawks play at the United ___
15 ___ Pilous was coach when Chicago won the Stanley Cup back in 1961

Mascot
"Tommy Hawk"

AHL Affiliate
Rockford IceHogs

ECHL Affiliate
Indy Fuel

FAST FACTS

Captain: **Jonathan Toews**

Coach: **Joel Quenneville**

GM: **Stan Bowman**

Arena: **United Center**

Capacity: **19,717**

Stanley Cups: **5**

Playoff Appearances: **59**

First Season: **1926-27**

GABRIEL LANDESKOG

THE LESSON GABRIEL LANDESKOG LEARNED and still abides by is simple: no risk, no reward. He could've played things much safer on his path to becoming a professional hockey player. He could've waited until he was older and more physically mature before trying to turn pro player in his native Sweden. But when he was 16 years and 90 days old he became the youngest person ever to play for Djurgarden of the Swedish League.

Gabriel could've earned good money as a teenager in the SHL, but he chose instead to move on to Canada at 16 to play major junior hockey, where the pay is much lower but the route to the NHL is more direct. He went on to be named the first European-born captain of the Ontario League's Kitchener Rangers.

In fact, Gabriel later became the youngest captain in NHL history when the Colorado Avalanche gave him that title Sept. 4, 2012. He was 19 years, 286 days old – 11 days earlier than the previous record-holder, Sidney Crosby of the Pittsburgh Penguins. It all looks so neat and easy, Gabriel's path to hockey's highest level. But it was his willingness to take risks on the roads less travelled that made it happen.

"I guess I've always been a little like that, not afraid to try new things, to look at life a little bit as an adventure," Gabriel said. "It's important when you're young to find something youre passionate about and really pursue it. For me, it was sports, mostly hockey."

Although Gabriel's father, Tony, was a former professional player in the Swedish leagues and a huge influence on his son's choice to become a hockey player, it was Gabriel's youth coach, Mattias Jonsson, who is responsible for much of his success. When he was about 10 years old, Gabriel played for a team coached by Jonsson, Hammarby, that was one of the top teams in his country for that age group.

"He made me realize that you can't just put in hard work when the team is practising," Gabriel said. "He said, 'The most important talent you have is when nobody's watching.' That hit home with me. Early nights, late mornings, stickhandling in the basement, whatever it might have been – you had to put in a lot of work to be successful, and he made me realize that."

Growing up in Stockholm, the capital of Sweden, there wasn't much NHL hockey to see on TV. But Jonsson would show NHL videos from the '70s and '80s to his team, and it was then that Gabriel began to dream of one day making it to North America to play in the best league in the world. His father had

> ## IT'S IMPORTANT WHEN YOU'RE YOUNG TO FIND SOMETHING YOU'RE PASSIONATE ABOUT. FOR ME, IT WAS HOCKEY

92
GABRIEL
LANDESKOG
BORN: NOV. 23, 1992
HEIGHT: 6' 1"
WEIGHT: 204 lbs
POSITION: LW
SHOOTS: L

never played professionally outside of Sweden, but young Gabriel was determined.

"He was always practising day and night," Tony said. "He was always so committed to being the best he could possibly be. But he worked hard with his studies, too."

He wound up making Sweden's under-16 world juniors team, not to mention playing professionally for Djurgarden. Then came the big decision, at age 16, to jump to Canada and play for Kitchener. (He was originally drafted by the Plymouth Whalers, but his rights were traded to Kitchener).

"I had an opportunity to sign a contract in Sweden, but I was so curious about Canada and the lifestyle and the hockey," Gabriel said. "I wanted to make that transition to North American-style hockey sooner rather than right when you come into the NHL. I was sold right away after my visit to Kitchener. The only one I really had to convince was my mom, but after a couple of months she saw things my way."

Again, Gabriel's intuition and daring paid off. He impressed everyone, NHL scouts most of all, with his play in North America, and in 2011 the Avalanche chose him with the No. 2 pick overall, right behind Ryan Nugent-Hopkins.

Gabriel's first season, in 2011-12, went about as well as it could have. He played all 82 games, scoring 22 goals and adding 30 assists. He was rewarded with the Calder Trophy as the NHL's rookie of the year.

In 2013-14, Gabriel finally got a taste of some team success after poor records in his first two seasons with the Avalanche. As captain, he helped lead the Colorado to a Central Division championship, its first division title since 2003. The Avalanche lost in seven games to the Minnesota Wild in the first round of the playoffs, but Gabriel and the team know

MY FAVORITE...

Movie: *Gladiator*

TV show: *Friends*

Band: *Coldplay*

Meal: *Swedish meatballs and spaghetti*

Store: *Ikea*

Thing I can't do without: *Good earphones on the plane rides*

Thing I like to do to teammates: *Photobombs*

brighter days are ahead. Having an accomplished captain who finished the season still only 21 is Exhibit A in that case.

"I'm lucky to be where I am," Gabriel said. "But I also know I worked hard for it." – **ADRIAN DATER**

Gabriel Landeskog

92

WORD SEARCH

JOE SAKIC
DENVER
J.S. GIGUERE
DUCHENE
ADAM FOOTE
IGINLA
MACKINNON
PEPSI
PATRICK ROY
LANDESKOG
NORDIQUES
ROCKIES
O'REILLY
SHERMAN

K	S	T	I	G	I	N	L	A	N	E	D	P
Y	A	D	A	M	F	O	O	T	E	M	E	C
D	E	M	L	E	U	R	K	U	M	P	L	S
N	N	P	I	R	O	D	L	S	S	A	E	N
J	O	E	S	A	K	I	C	I	L	T	T	L
S	N	E	H	L	G	Q	A	Y	N	R	A	A
G	N	Y	E	S	O	U	H	O	Q	I	L	N
I	I	C	R	E	F	E	N	E	H	C	U	D
G	K	X	M	I	R	S	P	D	E	K	O	E
U	C	U	A	K	S	O	U	A	W	R	N	S
E	A	V	N	C	K	N	Z	R	S	O	I	K
R	M	P	O	O	R	E	I	L	L	Y	N	O
E	A	S	J	R	E	V	N	E	D	K	M	G

→ My First
GAME

October 8, 2011
Detroit Red Wings **3**
@ Colorado Avalanche **0**
5 shots, 16:03 ice time

GABRIEL
LANDESKOG

"I don't have many great memories of how my first game went, but I still have a lot of great memories of how it felt. Putting on that real home uniform for the first time, taking the ice for that first shift, it was real special and exciting. I also have good memories of seeing one of my heroes, Peter Forsberg, get his number retired by the Avs before my first game. He was a huge star in Sweden and with the Avs, someone I really looked up to as a kid, and here I was, shaking his hand."

CROSSWORD

ACROSS

1 ___ Varlamov, pictured, is in goal in Colorado
3 Tyson ___ is a blueliner with the Avalanche
7 Where a team like the Avs stays when on the road
8 Captain ___ Landeskog is from Sweden
9 Winger ___ McLeod
11 Puck
14 Properly perform a play
16 Patrick Roy is now ___ in Colorado
17 Maxime ___ is a center with the Avs
18 The Avalanche play at the Pepsi ___

DOWN

1 Roy won the Conn ___ Trophy three times
2 Ryan ___ is coming off a big season with the Avalanche
4 Colorado's first NHL team went by this nickname
5 Stands out
6 ___ Sherman is GM in Colorado
10 Nathan MacKinnon was drafted first ___ in 2013
11 Matt ___ is also coming off a big season with the Avs
12 Andre ___ is on defense in Colorado
13 Black eye
15 Defenseman ___ Johnson was drafted first overall in 2006

Mascot
"Bernie the St. Bernard"

AHL Affiliate
Lake Erie Monsters

ECHL Affiliate
Fort Wayne Komets

FAST FACTS

Captain: **Gabriel Landeskog**

Coach: **Patrick Roy**

GM: **Greg Sherman**

Arena: **Pepsi Center**

Capacity: **18,007**

Stanley Cups: **2**

Playoff Appearances: **22**

First Season: **1979-80**

RYAN JOHANSEN

RYAN JOHANSEN IS ONLY 22 YEARS OLD, BUT his career is already a lesson in perseverance. He had a breakout season in 2013-14, leading the Columbus Blue Jackets with 33 goals and 63 points and helping the franchise reach the playoffs for only the second time in its 13-season history.

It's hard to imagine one of the NHL's budding superstars – Ryan was 11th in the league in goals in 2013-14 – struggling to put up points in his first two seasons. Not if you know his history, however.

"I guess I'm just a slow starter," Ryan said, with a shrug and a laugh.

In 2007, Ryan wasn't picked until the seventh round, No. 150 overall, in the bantam draft by the Western League's Portland Winterhawks. Instead of joining them the next fall, he played in the British Columbia League to maintain his U.S. college eligibility, because he'd been offered a scholarship at Northeastern University in Boston, Mass.

But even his Jr. A career with Penticton didn't come with an easy start. Ryan was a healthy scratch so many times early in 2008-09 that the Vees' staff taught him how to use the video camera to record game nights so the team could watch it before practice the following day.

"I was so young and so happy just to be part of a team like that," Ryan said. "I really wanted to play, of course. Everybody wants to play. But I don't remember being as dejected by it as I probably should have been. I didn't have to do it as much in the second part of the season."

Ryan became a regular for Penticton, but his numbers didn't suggest star potential. He had five goals and 12 assists in 47 games that season.

"We had him on the fourth line early in the season, when he played," said Fred Harbison, Penticton's coach. "But we kept giving him more and more, and he kept playing better and better, with more confidence. That's the big thing with Ryan and so many other kids. They have to develop confidence, and his just soared as the season went on. By the playoffs, he was getting top-six time and power play time, and he might have been our best player at the end of the season."

Ryan hasn't held a video camera since, he joked. He moved on to Portland the next season, and had 25 goals, 44 assists and a plus-17 rating in 71 games.

"I started to see what I could do that year in Penticton," Ryan said. "And it motivated me to do even more, and I just kept getting rewarded for it and realizing what more I could do. When you start

> **RYAN GOT AN OPPORTUNITY THIS SEASON, AND INSTEAD OF WALKING THROUGH THE DOOR HE KNOCKED IT OVER**

to get a taste like that, it's really exciting. It's the reward for hard work."

Just three years after he was selected with the 150th overall pick in the bantam draft, Ryan went No. 4 overall in the NHL draft. The Blue Jackets surprised many by taking him so early, but then-GM Scott Howson saw Ryan as a similar player to the San Jose Sharks' Joe Thornton, who was Ryan's idol when he was growing up in Port Moody, B.C.

"He's the reason I wear No. 19," Ryan said.

Ryan had to climb the ladder again when he arrived in the NHL. He was played on the fourth line, made a healthy scratch and sent to the American League five times in his first two seasons while Columbus waited for his skill set to emerge.

"We're invested in him," said coach Todd Richards. "We demanded that he play the game the right way, and it took some time to teach him that 200-foot game, not just this night or that night, but every night. But he got an opportunity this season, and instead of walking through the door he knocked it over."

Ryan led the Blue Jackets in goals (33), points (63), game-winning goals (five), shots on goal (237), faceoff wins (692) and shootout goals (three). He was second in shifts (1,847). His production was a pleasant surprise for the Blue Jackets but not to Minnesota Wild forward Nino Niederreiter, who was Ryan's linemate back in Portland.

"Ryan is a really laid-back guy," Niederreiter said. "But he wants to win. He wants to be great."

Ryan knows he still has more work to do.

"For years, I heard people talk about my potential, what I was going to be," he said. "It's nice to deliver on that, but I still feel like I have a lot to learn and a long way to go. And that's exciting."

— AARON PORTZLINE

MY FAVORITE...

Movie: *Happy Gilmore*

TV show: *Suits*

Band: *The 1975*

Celebrity: *Jim Carrey*

Video game: *Halo*

Pre-game meal: *Pasta and chicken*

Junk food: *Ice cream*

Vacation destination: *Whistler, B.C.*

Player growing up: *Joe Thornton*

Team growing up: *Vancouver*

Sport other than hockey: *Golf*

Hockey memory: *2010 world juniors*

Way to score: *Breakaway*

WORD SEARCH

RICHARDS
OHIO
RICK NASH
JOHANSEN
DUBINSKY
LETESTU
SPRINGFIELD
STINGER
VEZINA
KEKALAINEN
BOBROVSKY
METROPOLITAN
KLESLA
NATIONWIDE

B	N	S	J	O	R	I	C	K	N	A	S	H
Y	D	T	R	T	L	K	L	E	S	L	A	C
V	L	A	L	P	U	R	K	D	D	C	B	S
R	E	G	N	I	T	S	E	I	R	M	O	N
E	I	Z	K	E	N	A	K	W	A	I	B	Y
J	F	U	I	S	G	V	A	N	H	X	R	K
O	G	Y	T	N	O	N	L	O	C	O	O	S
H	N	C	O	S	A	H	A	I	I	R	V	N
A	I	X	N	N	E	E	I	T	R	A	S	I
N	R	U	A	U	S	T	N	A	W	I	K	B
S	P	V	L	D	K	N	E	N	S	H	Y	U
E	S	P	O	U	E	D	N	L	D	E	N	D
N	A	T	I	L	O	P	O	R	T	E	M	H

My First GAME

October 7, 2011
Nashville Predators 3
@ C. Blue Jackets 2
8:46 ice time

RYAN
JOHANSEN

"Honestly, I barely remember the game. I don't really have any details of it, other than we lost at home against Nashville. My mind was just everywhere. The only vivid memory I have is being on the bench at the start of the game and looking across the ice and seeing my family across the stands. It just kind of hit me then, that I'd made it, that my dream had come true. The only thing I kept was the framed scoresheet from the NHL that they give every player when they make their NHL debut."

CROSSWORD

ACROSS

1 Ryan ___ is on defense
3 Todd Richards took over for Scott ___ as coach
7 Unmarked
8 Nick ___, pictured, is a winger
9 Some fans arrive early at the rink to watch the team ___ up
11 The Blue Jackets visit Montreal's ___ Centre a couple times each season
14 Columbus is now in the NHL's ___ Conference
16 Nationwide ___ is where the Blue Jackets play their home games
17 Quickly score in response to an opponent's goal
18 Not fair

DOWN

1 The Blue Jackets traded ___ Gaborik to L.A. for Matt Frattin and some high draft picks
2 James Wisniewski spent a season here earlier in his career
4 Against the rules
5 Both Boone Jenner and Curtis McElhinney hail from here
6 No. 8 Across's father, Mike, was a Sabre and a Maple ___
10 No. 15 Down racked up a team record 258 ___ while with Columbus
11 ___ Dubinsky
12 Sergei Bobrovsky won the ___ Trophy in 2013
13 Wisniewski hails from ___, Mich.
15 Former captain Rick ___ was drafted first overall in 2002

Mascot
"Stinger"

AHL Affiliate
Springfield Falcons

ECHL Affiliate
Evansville IceMen

STARS

JAMIE BENN

AS A KID, JAMIE BENN HAD A LITTLE HELP CON- juring dreams of the NHL. The Benn household in Victoria, B.C., didn't produce just one NHL player, but two. Jamie and Jordie have both made their careers in professional hockey, and the two are teammates on the Dallas Stars.

"You really couldn't ask for anything more," Jamie said. "You dream of growing up and playing in the NHL, but to do it with your brother, that's pretty special."

At 27, Jordie is two years older and a great leader, according to his kid brother. Jamie, as the elder brother tells it, is a natural athlete and a great competitor. As kids, they found a way to play sports most of the time.

"They were pretty competitive," said their dad, Randy Benn. "They were always playing some sort of game and usually playing it pretty hard."

Randy established a strong base. He played softball internationally for Canada, winning gold medals in the 1976 World Championship and the 1979 Pan Am Games. The Benn boys were known just as much on Vancouver Island for their baseball exploits as they were for hockey.

Still, it was Canada, and it was hockey, so there was a special intensity as the games unfolded in the street or the garage. Jamie was typically Joe Sakic, the pride of Burnaby, B.C., and a local hero well worth imitating. Jordie, a huge Canucks fan, was often Trevor Linden or Ed Jovanovski.

"You're kids, that's what you do," Jordie said. "Every game was Game 7. Every game, the Stanley Cup was on the line. It was great. You need those dreams to push you and keep you going."

Jordie admits it took him a while to believe in the NHL dream. He didn't play major junior and went undrafted. He followed Jamie to Texas and made the most of his opportunities there. He played one season with the Allen Americans of the Central League. That led Jordie to the Texas Stars, Dallas' American League affiliate, where he played 165 games over three seasons. In 2013-14, he earned his way into Dallas' lineup, perhaps for good.

"You look at how hard he has worked, how he has forced his way onto the roster, and it's an inspiration, really," said Jim Nill, general manager of the Dallas Stars. "He was a six or seven (defenseman on the depth chart) going into the season and now he's a top four."

Jamie has excelled at a much quicker pace, but he's also had to prove himself. As a fifth-round NHL

> YOU DREAM OF GROWING UP AND PLAYING IN THE NHL, BUT TO DO IT WITH YOUR BROTHER, THAT'S PRETTY AMAZING

14

JAMIE
BENN
BORN: JULY 18, 1989
HEIGHT: 6' 2"
WEIGHT: 210 lbs
POSITION: LW
SHOOTS: L

draft pick, Jamie helped push the Kelowna Rockets of the Western League to the Memorial Cup final in 2009 and then carried the Texas Stars to the American League's Calder Cup final in 2010. His 2013-14 season was an indication of how he embraces a challenge and doesn't mind proving himself to others. He wasn't included on Canada's orientation camp roster for the Winter Olympics but ended up making the team.

"He was left off of Canada's list and worked his way onto that list," said Lindy Ruff, coach of the Dallas Stars and an assistant coach with Team Canada. "He started at the bottom at the Olympics with just getting into a game, and then he worked his way into important minutes. Those are all tremendous accomplishments on his part. It's his determination. He's a fearless player."

The Benn boys say their determination was built in a household where "belief" was a key word. Jordie said his father pushed him and supported him. While it would have been easy for Jordie to give up on the hockey dream, Randy kept telling him to dig in, to work harder, to never quit. It was a message so strong that Jordie had the phrase "Never Quit" tattooed onto his left bicep. Jamie got "Benn" tattooed on his arm. For both, their family upbringing has a lot to do with why they're here now.

"The fact that we were allowed to share that dream and push for it – I definitely think that's one of the reasons we were able to make it," Jamie said. "I don't think either of us were seriously saying, 'Let's go play in the NHL,' but we wanted to be the best, and that's important. We were just kids having fun, but part of the fun was making each other better and pushing as hard as we could."

It's an uncommon tale, but one the Benn brothers believe can be shared by others. If you are truly

MY FAVORITE...

Movie: **Slap Shot**

TV show: **Game of Thrones**

Musician: **I like all sorts of music, mostly country**

Concert: **Kenny Chesney at Cowboys Stadium**

Car: **Bentley Continental Supersport**

Pre-game tradition: **Starbucks and Bran Flakes**

Meal: **A steak dinner**

Player growing up: **Joe Sakic**

Player in another sport: **Ken Griffey Jr.**

pushing toward your dream, it's a good idea to have someone racing beside you.

"I always wanted to do what he did when I was a kid," Jamie said. "I always wanted to be where he was. He was a great role model for me to follow."

And vice versa. – **MIKE HEIKA**

WORD SEARCH

NICHUSHKIN

EAKIN

HITCHCOCK

BROTEN

JAMIE BENN

WHITNEY

JIM NILL

MIKE MODANO

LINDY RUFF

SEGUIN

TEXAS

LEHTONEN

TURCO

MINNESOTA

D	M	A	U	M	U	T	O	L	V	E	O	T
H	I	T	C	H	C	O	C	K	R	S	U	E
N	K	O	N	J	L	E	P	A	J	R	E	X
I	E	S	E	A	K	I	N	Y	C	O	P	A
K	M	E	S	M	N	E	T	O	R	B	L	S
H	O	N	S	I	Y	J	A	U	B	I	E	E
S	D	N	E	E	E	L	J	N	R	Y	H	F
U	A	I	A	B	G	I	T	R	O	E	T	E
H	N	M	V	E	M	U	S	I	U	N	O	R
C	O	G	Q	N	M	H	I	Z	G	T	N	S
I	I	T	I	N	R	U	T	N	H	I	E	Y
N	N	L	S	I	R	A	P	H	C	H	N	Q
I	L	I	N	D	Y	R	U	F	F	W	D	K

→ *My First*
GAME

October 3, 2009
*Nashville Predators **3**
@ Dallas Stars **2** (SO)
2 shots, 15:59 ice time*

JAMIE
BENN

"*I remember there was a lot of excitement surrounding my first game, because it was the first game of the season. We had a full house, and everyone was nervous before the game. I was nervous and excited, and I couldn't wait to get out there. I think I played with Mike Ribeiro and Brenden Morrow or maybe with Mike Modano, but I know it was strange to look over and see them on the ice. It went so fast. I remember after my first shift sitting on the bench and thinking, 'OK, now I've played in the NHL.'*"

CROSSWORD

ACROSS

1 ___ Nichushkin is a Russian-born Star

3 Former Bruins Tim Thomas and No. 17 Across were both acquired by the Stars in ___

7 Dallas is in this state

8 Shawn ___, pictured, was previously an Oiler

9 Missing

11 The Stars met this team when they went on the road for the first time in 2013-14

14 A goalie who is very nimble and flops around a lot may be likened to this circus performer

16 A ___ penalty is five minutes

17 Tyler ___ was drafted second overall by Boston in 2010

18 Flyers great Bob ___ was briefly Stars GM

DOWN

1 Goes on the road

2 Antoine ___ is on the wing

4 Where No. 11 Down worked before coming to Dallas

5 Dissension

6 ___ Peverley was also a Bruin

10 Coach Lindy Ruff hails from this Alberta town

11 Dallas Stars GM

12 Ruff previously coached this team

13 No. 2 Down is one of few NHLers to come from this country

15 The Stars had a whopping 22 ___ back in 1969-70

AHL Affiliate
Texas Stars

ECHL Affiliate
Idaho Steelheads

FAST FACTS

Captain: ***Jamie Benn***

Coach: ***Lindy Ruff***

GM: ***Jim Nill***

Arena: ***American Airlines Center***

Capacity: ***18,532***

Stanley Cups: ***1***

Playoff Appearances: ***30***

First Season: ***1967-68***

HENRIK ZETTERBERG

WHEN HE LOOKS AROUND THE DETROIT RED Wings' dressing room at the wide-eyed children of his teammates, whether it's Johan Franzen's son playfully trying on Jimmy Howard's mask or Daniel Alfredsson's boys excitedly chasing a tennis ball with their mini-sticks, Henrik Zetterberg is instantly reminded of his own childhood hockey fantasy.

As a wee lad back home in Sweden, Henrik frequently tagged along at his father Goran's side when his dad went to work as a hockey player with Njurunda of the Swedish League's second division.

"Following him to practice and being in the locker room, I knew I wanted to be a hockey player, too," Henrik said. "I saw my dad going out and skating, and that's when I realized that this is something I want to do."

Henrik, the captain of the Red Wings, won an Olympic gold medal with Sweden in 2006 and was the Conn Smythe Trophy winner as playoff MVP when Detroit captured the Stanley Cup in the spring of 2008. And as much as he's known for his tremendous skill on the ice, Henrik is very much the epitome of the fearless competitor. It's a trait he believes evolved when he was a youngster. He was slower to develop physically than many of his best buddies and on-ice opponents.

> IT WAS TOUGH WHEN I WAS STILL A LITTLE KID AND ALL THE OTHERS WERE BIGGER AND STRONGER

"I was kind of a late bloomer," Henrik said. "For a couple of years there, it was a little tough when I was still a little kid and all the others were bigger and stronger."

He was a little man, but had a big heart, and that's what kept him going.

"A lot of it had to do with the fact that I was really small growing up," Henrik said. "I really had to find ways to compete with other guys who were a lot bigger than me. I was always playing against bigger guys. You had to find ways to handle that. Once you caught up strength-wise, you had that determination already. It definitely helped me to get better."

Still undersized by professional standards, Henrik was often overlooked when NHL scouts came looking for prospects, but in Sweden he was slowly gaining traction within the national team program.

In 1997-98, he was selected to the Swedish under-18 team that played in the European championship. His offensive numbers (three points in six games) were limited, however, and Henrik was overshadowed by the Sedin twins, Henrik and Daniel. They were the story, not only in Swedish circles but across the hockey world, with their incredible skill and uncanny sense for finding each other on the ice.

MY FAVORITE...

TV Show: *Seinfeld*

Musician: *Bob Dylan*

Video game: *I don't play video games that much*

Pre-game meal: *Chicken with pasta*

Junk food: *Sibylla. It's a Swedish hamburger restaurant*

Player growing up: *Wayne Gretzky*

Sport other than hockey: *Golf*

Hockey memory: *Winning the Stanley Cup in 2008*

Way to score: *Don't have one. Just as long as it goes in*

Although he wasn't on the radar at that time, Henrik won many fans in the Swedish dressing room for his willingness to sacrifice and do the dirty work at both ends of the rink.

"The way he plays now, he did that when he was younger, too," said Detroit defenseman Niklas Kronwall, who first met Henrik when they played for that under-18 team. " 'Hank' was our second-line center who did everything right. You could always tell his determination, but at the time it was hard to see that he was going to be as good as he is today."

The Wings rolled the dice on Henrik, selected him 210th overall in the 1999 draft, and before long that gamble would pay dividends.

Henrik broke into the Swedish League with Timra in 2000-01 and was named the league's top rookie. In 2002, he was one of two non-NHLers selected to the Swedish team for the 2002 Salt Lake City Winter Olympics.

"Definitely, that was a moment – I still call it later in my career, but really, it was early – when I really noticed that, OK, I can play with these guys," Henrik said.

He came to Detroit in 2002, and no one back home was surprised when Henrik earned a spot on the 2002-03 NHL all-rookie team.

"He was the captain for his pro team back home at a very early age, and guys don't get that 'C' without having that drive," Kronwall said. "Just his attitude and his will to compete and really become better every year, that's what set him apart from the other guys. He outworks the other guys."

Henrik is living proof that just because you're little, it doesn't mean you can't go a long way. – **BOB DUFF**

Henrik Zetterberg

40

WORD SEARCH

ZETTERBERG
LIDSTROM
JOE LOUIS
SAWCHUK
BABCOCK
DATSYUK
HOLLAND
OCTOPUS
DELVECCHIO
YZERMAN
KRONWALL
ALFREDSSON
HOWE
LINDSAY

```
H H R G R E B R E T T E Z
T J D E L V E C C H I O L
W Y A S D N I L A N N W L
E E T R V K C O C B A B A
L L S A W C H U K B L Y W
I T Y Z U B H Y N D F A N
D V U Z T Z R O F K R M O
S I K A E D R P W S E O R
T S N Z E R M U T E D M K
R U O H O V M S S T S N S
O J R H O L L A N D S P S
M S U P O T C O N C O Z H
Y J J O E L O U I S I N A I
```

My First
GAME

October 10, 2002
Detroit Red Wings 6
@ San Jose Sharks 3
1 A, 14:57 ice time

HENRIK
ZETTERBERG

"I don't really recall my first NHL game nearly as well as the first NHL game I saw in person. The Wings flew Niklas Kronwall and me to Detroit to watch the 2002 Western Conference final series against the Colorado Avalanche. The intensity on the ice was incredible. 'Kronner' and I, we looked at each other and said, 'No, no, no, we can't do this next year.' The next fall, I debuted in a 6-3 win over the San Jose Sharks. I got clocked by (defenseman) Scott Hannan in the corner first shift. That's the biggest memory I have."

CROSSWORD

ACROSS

1 ___ Kronwall is alternate captain in Detroit and generally pairs with Jonathan Ericsson
3 Mike ___ is the Wings' owner
7 Give out
8 One who suits up every night (like Kronwall did in 2012-13, when he played every game)
9 ___ Ullman was part of the deal that made a Red Wing of Frank Mahovlich
11 The trophy won six times by Gordie Howe
14 Howe was also the last Red Wing to win this trophy
16 Gustav Nyquist is one, as is No. 12 down
17 'Terrible Ted' Lindsay won the ___ Patrick Trophy
18 Petr ___ is one of the Wings' backup goalies

DOWN

1 Nicklas Lidstrom is a seven-time ___ Trophy winner
2 Mike Babcock coached here before coming to Detroit
4 One who follows the main action of a play
5 Jimmy ___, pictured, is between the pipes in Detroit
6 Jakub Kindl's number
10 Item that often gets tossed on the ice at Joe Louis
11 Player who goes all out all the time, like Lindsay did
12 ___ Alfredsson signed with Detroit as a free agent in 2013
13 ___ Zetterberg wears the 'C'
15 Alfie's former team

Mascot
"Al the Octopus"

AHL Affiliate
Grand Rapids Griffins

ECHL Affiliate
Toledo Walleye

TAYLOR HALL

SURE, EDMONTON OILERS LEFT WINGER TAYLOR Hall was pushed around in a sled as a youngster, but you wouldn't find him zipping down the chute at the same speeds his father did with the Canadian national team.

"You had to be a certain age to go down the bobsleigh track," Taylor said. "And by that time, I was too serious about hockey for me to go risking my life."

So instead of flying down an icy hill, Taylor decided to continue soaring across sheets of ice.

Taylor's father, Steve Hall, played in the Canadian Football League before turning his interests to bobsleigh. Living in Calgary, he had the facilities he needed thanks to the 1988 Winter Olympics. Taylor's passion, however, had always been in hockey.

"My memories are of him just always wanting to go play," said Taylor's mom, Kim Strba. "His father built a rink in the backyard every winter, and the kids in the neighborhood would all come over every day. That's the type of unorganized hockey where they can get very creative."

Which has clearly paid off in the long run for Taylor. Since he joined the Ontario League as a 15-year-old, Taylor has been dazzling folks with his great skill and goal-scoring ability. Funny to think, then,

IT COULD HAVE BEEN MAKE-OR-BREAK FOR A TEENAGE BOY, BUT TAYLOR HANDLED IT VERY WELL

how major junior history might have changed if the Hall family had remained in Calgary and Taylor got drafted into the Western League.

But as it was, Taylor, then 13, moved with his family to Kingston, Ont., where Kim's six brothers and sisters lived. It was a different experience for him as a teen, but he got to Kingston on a Thursday and had a team and a new best friend by Friday. Still, it was tough saying goodbye to Calgary.

"He didn't want to go," Kim said. "He took one for the team there. It could have been make-or-break for a teenage boy, but he handled it very well."

In Kingston, his game continued to grow and soon Taylor was on to the OHL's Windsor Spitfires. Being born in November, he was still 15 when his OHL experience began, but that didn't stop him from making an immediate impact. The Spitfires were beginning to come on as a juggernaut, and Taylor did his share by pumping in 45 goals as a freshman, leading the team in that category. Not too shabby, considering that the Spits also featured Josh Bailey, who rang up 96 points that campaign before eventually becoming a New York Islander.

The next season, Windsor rode Taylor, defenseman Ryan Ellis and Calgary Flames pick Greg

Nemisz all the way to the Memorial Cup. The Spitfires returned to the junior championship the following season as well, trouncing the host Brandon Wheat Kings 9-1 in the title match.

"Maybe the second one was more gratifying," Taylor said, "because we won so convincingly."

Taylor went No. 1 overall in the 2010 draft, joining a young Edmonton Oilers squad that included fellow rookie Jordan Eberle, a teammate from the world juniors. Although he had just one assist in his first seven games, Taylor followed up with multi-point efforts in the next two outings, including his first NHL goal in a game against Columbus. But it was those same Blue Jackets who would put a serious cramp in Taylor's rookie season.

On March 3, 2011, after having already tallied a goal and an assist, he got into an ill-advised fight with Columbus' tough guy Derek Dorsett. Taylor fell awkwardly in the tilt and injured his ankle. On the bright side, it marked his first Gordie Howe hat trick. The downsides, however, were much greater. The season was finished for Taylor, just as he was putting together a run of offense.

"I don't think he was really expecting what (the NHL) was going to be like," Eberle said. "As the year went on, he got really good. He was playing his best hockey until he got injured, which sucked because he would have kept playing really well."

Along the way, Taylor has always gotten advice from his father. With Steve withstanding the rigors of the CFL schedule and excelling in bobsleigh, he knew what his son needed to do to succeed. And although they played different sports, Taylor always listened to what his father had to say about his performance on the ice.

"It's pretty hard to see yourself when you're playing," Taylor said. "So it was great having him there."

MY FAVORITE...

Movie: *Good Will Hunting*

Cartoon: *Hey Arnold!*

Album: *Theory of a Deadman by Theory of a Deadman*

Junk Food: *McDonald's*

Jersey: *Team Canada*

Memorabilia: *Signed Bobby Orr jersey*

School Subject: *Geography*

Taylor's mom also saw the importance of having another elite athlete in the family as her son grew up.

"He saw the dedication that Steve had for his sport," Kim said. "And the passion, that's something you can't teach." **– RYAN KENNEDY**

WORD SEARCH

ALBERTA
FERENCE
SCRIVENS
EBERLE
REXALL
GRETZKY
POCKLINGTON
TAYLOR HALL
MESSIER
EAKINS
RYAN SMYTH
MAC 'T'
GRANT FUHR
COFFEY

R	Y	A	N	S	M	Y	T	H	V	E	O	T
H	K	T	P	H	S	O	A	K	G	S	U	D
N	Z	Q	O	J	E	E	Y	A	R	L	E	X
I	T	S	C	F	C	C	L	Y	A	U	P	A
K	E	A	K	I	N	S	O	O	N	E	L	M
H	R	N	L	G	E	J	R	F	T	L	E	E
A	G	P	I	D	R	L	H	C	F	R	H	F
L	A	I	N	B	E	I	A	R	U	E	T	L
B	N	M	G	E	F	M	L	I	H	B	Y	L
E	O	G	T	A	U	H	L	Z	R	E	N	A
R	I	T	O	N	P	U	T	N	H	I	E	X
T	N	S	N	E	V	I	R	C	S	H	N	E
A	L	Y	N	D	O	M	E	S	S	I	E	R

My First
GAME

October 7, 2010
Calgary Flames **0**
@ Edmonton Oilers **4**
4 shots, 16:59 ice time

TAYLOR
HALL

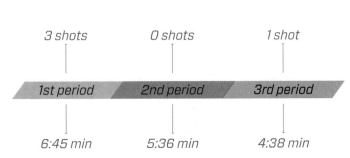

3 shots	0 shots	1 shot
1st period	2nd period	3rd period
6:45 min	5:36 min	4:38 min

CROSSWORD

ACROSS

1 ___ Eberle is an alternate captain in Edmonton
3 Mark Messier was the first Oiler to win the Conn ___ Trophy
7 Ben ___ saw limited duty with the Oilers in 2013-14
8 Nationality of Nail Yakupov
9 The abbreviation for the National Collegiate Athletic Association
11 Back part of the skate boot (or what your dog may do)
14 Wayne Gretzky amassed an amazing 1,086 ___ as an Oiler
16 The Oilers play at Rexall ___
17 Where Eberle hails from
18 They show you to your seat

DOWN

1 Sweater
2 When the Flames and Oilers clash, it's the 'Battle of ___'
4 Gretzky was a ___-___ winner of the trophy referred to in No. 3 Across
5 Dallas ___ is behind the bench in Edmonton
6 Number worn by Taylor Hall
10 Making the most of a scoring opportunity, ___ in
11 Ryan Nugent-___, pictured, was drafted first overall in 2011
12 Former Oiler Sam ___ is from London, Ont.
13 No. 11 Down played his junior hockey with the Red Deer ___
15 2002 Olympic host ___ Lake City is also the hometown of former Oilers goalie Richard Bachman

---

AHL Affiliate
Oklahoma City Barons

ECHL Affiliate
Bakersfield Condors

FAST FACTS

Captain: **Andrew Ference**

Coach: **Dallas Eakins**

GM: **Craig MacTavis**

Arena: **Rexall Place**

Capacity: **16,839**

Stanley Cups: **5**

Playoff Appearances: **20**

First Season: **1979-80**

JONATHAN HUBERDEAU

JONATHAN HUBERDEAU HASN'T HAD TO FACE A lot of adversity as a hockey player. Usually the best player on whatever team he was on, he found the competition a bit stiffer when he arrived at his first training camp with the Florida Panthers in 2011. But even then, he excelled.

Jonathan led the Panthers in scoring during his first training camp, scoring three goals in six pre-season games, but Florida still decided he wasn't ready for the rigors of 82 games in the NHL. General manager Dale Tallon made the tough decision to send Huberdeau back to his junior team in Saint John, N.B., even though he knew his rookie left winger was good enough to make an impact at the NHL level.

"He's a really good player," said teammate Tomas Kopecky. "A guy who is going to be a star in this league."

The Panthers just didn't want to rush things. Jonathan, Tallon said, needed another year of seasoning. Another year of dominating the Quebec League, another trip to the world juniors, another year to get stronger, not only physically but mentally as well.

"I had a great camp," Jonathan said. "I was scoring goals, but I knew I wasn't ready. I had no regrets. Maybe I would have been upset had I not done all I could. I gave it my all."

As a kid, Jonathan moved through the minor hockey ranks until he was selected by Saint John with the 18th-overall pick in the 2009 QMJHL draft. In four seasons with the Sea Dogs, Jonathan was a scoring machine, recording 104 goals and 257 points in 195 games. In 2010-11, he scored 43 goals and helped lead Saint John to the Memorial Cup. In the Memorial Cup final, he had a goal and an assist to help the Sea Dogs beat Mississauga 3-1 to earn MVP honors.

"I got there when I was 16 and had to learn a new language," Jonathan said. "It was a great time for me. We had a great team, great bunch of guys. I was far from home, but I wasn't homesick."

Not long after Jonathan's Memorial Cup heroics, Florida selected him with the third-overall pick in the 2011 draft. It was a homecoming of sorts. Although Huberdeau grew up in Quebec and was raised on the Montreal Canadiens, the Panthers were his second-favorite team.

Around Christmas each year, he and his family drove south in the family Winnebago and hung out near the Panthers' arena in Sunrise. The trip coincided with the Florida's annual holiday series, in which the Canadiens were one of the visiting teams.

> I NEVER THOUGHT, SITTING UP IN THOSE STANDS AS A KID, THAT I'D BE ON THE ICE PLAYING FOR THE PANTHERS

11

JONATHAN
HUBERDEAU
BORN: JUNE 4, 1993
HEIGHT: 6' 1"
WEIGHT: 188 lbs
POSITION: LW
SHOOTS: L

Jonathan laughs at the memories of watching those games as a young spectator. A large mural of him wearing his red Panthers gear now greets fans entering the same arena where he once cheered for the visiting team.

"I used to come down here and cheer against the Panthers, so to be here now, it's pretty cool," Jonathan said. "I never thought, sitting up in those stands as a kid, that I would be down on the ice playing for the Panthers."

Although Jonathan didn't make the team immediately after being drafted, there was little doubt he'd be with the club the following season. Of course, the NHL lockout postponed his big-league debut. Jonathan stayed in Saint John for the first half of 2012-13 (he had 45 points in 30 games) and represented Team Canada at the world juniors again that December. When the lockout finally ended, Jonathan was summoned to South Florida. He didn't expect to go back to junior, and never did.

On Jan. 19, 2013, Huberdeau officially made his NHL debut. It was an exciting night for both him and his teammates as the team's Southeast Division championship banner from 2011-12 was raised to the rafters. Huberdeau scored a goal on his first shot on his second shift of the game, and Florida opened the season with a 5-1 win over the Carolina Hurricanes.

"He came in that following year after playing in Saint John, and he was a step ahead of everyone," said then-Florida coach Kevin Dineen. "That translated into what was a special first game as well as a special rookie season. He was ready to go for us."

Jonathan had 14 goals and 17 assists playing in all 48 of Florida's games in 2012-13. When the season was done, he was honored as the franchise's first winner of the rookie of the year award. It was quite a

MY FAVORITE...

Movie: *Coach Carter*

TV show: *Breaking Bad*

Celebrity: *Katy Perry. She's my crush*

Musician: *Justin Timberlake*

Player growing up: *Mario Lemieux*

Team growing up: *Montreal Canadiens*

Pregame meal: *Chicken and pasta*

Junk food: *Hooters chicken wings*

Video game: *EA NHL*

Sport other than hockey: *Tennis*

Hockey memories: *Being drafted, 1st NHL goal*

Way to score a goal: *R-to-L in the shootout*

year, one that turned out to be worth waiting for.

"I didn't think about winning the Calder Trophy as the season was going on," Jonathan said. "I just wanted to make a good impression on the Panthers. I thought I made a statement by playing as well as I could. I got off to a great start, but I then went cold for a time. I had to battle that. I learned that things in the NHL could go up and they could go down. But it's been good so far." **- GEORGE RICHARDS**

WORD SEARCH

DALE TALLON
LUONGO
GALLANT
WEISS
STANLEY C.
JOKINEN
MACLEAN
SUNRISE
HUBERDEAU
SKRUDLAND
BRAD BOYES
BOLLAND
UPSHALL
JOVANOVSKI

B	S	S	J	O	C	H	E	A	N	E	D	M
Y	L	T	B	O	L	L	A	N	D	M	A	H
D	N	A	L	D	U	R	K	S	M	C	L	S
N	A	N	I	O	O	D	L	S	L	I	E	N
E	R	L	K	E	N	A	L	E	L	L	T	U
N	L	E	S	S	G	T	A	Y	N	H	A	A
I	S	Y	V	I	O	N	H	O	Q	Y	L	E
K	F	C	O	R	E	A	S	B	T	R	L	D
O	E	X	N	N	R	L	P	D	E	W	O	R
J	T	U	A	U	S	L	U	A	W	Z	N	E
E	L	V	V	S	K	A	Z	R	S	H	I	B
Y	F	P	O	U	E	G	L	B	D	E	N	U
K	A	S	J	I	W	E	I	S	S	K	M	H

→ My First
GAME

January 19, 2013
Carolina Hurricanes **1**
@ Florida Panthers **5**
1 G, 2 A, first star

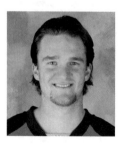

JONATHAN
HUBERDEAU

"It was like a dream and I was very excited about it. I just decided to go out and play my game. And then on my first shot in my second shift I scored. That was just a great moment. You don't realize how big it is to play in your first NHL game because it's been such a dream for so many years. You dream of that day, and then you score. I was just so happy. I saw the puck coming and it was like in slow motion. I was thinking, 'This is going to be your first NHL goal.' But it happened so quickly. It was a perfect game."

CROSSWORD

ACROSS

1 Jonathan Huberdeau hails from St. ___, Que.
3 Aleksander ___ is a Finn, as is Sean Bergenheim
7 Former Panthers goaltender 'Eddie the ___' Belfour
8 Glove worn by Roberto Luongo (and by all goalies)
9 Knock out
11 Something for Luongo to make (and he's made a lot)
14 Olli ___ was captain in Florida for four seasons
16 Defeat
17 Duane ___ had a short stint as Panthers coach
18 Ex-coach Horachek, and those with the same first name

DOWN

1 Scott Gomez, who signed with the Panthers in 2013-14, was previously with New ___
2 Doug ___ was the Panthers' second coach
4 Dmitry ___, pictured, is on defense in Florida
5 Players wear them to protect their eyes
6 Spear
10 To ___ ___ an opponent is to eliminate him with a solid check
11 ___ Upshall was among the team's top scorers in 2013-14
12 Tosses out
13 After being let go by the Panthers, Kevin Dineen went on to coach Canada's ___ team
15 Center ___ Bjugstad

Mascot
"Stanley C. Panther"

AHL Affiliate
San Antonio Rampage

ECHL Affiliate
Cincinnati Cyclones

FAST FACTS

Captain: *Vacant*

Coach: *Gerard Gallant*

GM: *Dale Tallon*

Arena: *BB&T Center*

Capacity: *19,250*

Stanley Cups: *0*

Playoff Appearances: *4*

First Season: *1993-94*

DREW DOUGHTY

DREW DOUGHTY IS REGARDED AS ONE OF THE NHL's top two-way defensemen. He was named after former Dallas Cowboys wide receiver Drew Pearson, one of the NFL's prime offensive threats of the '70s and '80s, and grew up playing goal in soccer.

"I learned a lot from playing goalie in soccer," Drew said. "I was able to read little things in front of me, and I learned to react. That's one of my strengths in hockey. I use my mind to try and read things before they happen."

Drew developed his love of hockey and soccer while growing up in a family of passionate sports fans in London, Ont. His father, Paul Doughty, played competitive soccer in Ontario after emigrating from England, and his sister, Chelsea, was named after fabled Chelsea F.C. of the European Premier League.

Drew is a big fan of both Chelseas. His sister plays soccer at Niagara University, and Drew keeps close tabs on her career. He also follows the team in the standings, checks out their highlights and watches games whenever his schedule permits.

Although Drew is making his name in hockey, soccer still runs in his blood. With a British-born father, and a mother, Connie, who hails from Portugal, Drew was born into a family that rallies around the sport,

> I LEARNED A LOT FROM PLAYING SOCCER. I READ LITTLE THINGS IN FRONT OF ME AND LEARNED TO REACT

and his early exposure to soccer has been an asset to his hockey career.

"Drew picked up on playing defense from watching me play soccer," Paul said. "When he first started playing hockey he was a center, but he was very defensive-minded for a forward."

In the summer of 2013, Drew spent part of his off-season visiting legendary soccer sites in England with his family. In addition to touring Chelsea F.C.'s home stadium, Stamford Bridge, the Doughtys visited Paul's hometown of Crawley, where they took in a game.

Hockey and soccer have always gone hand-in-hand for Drew, who grew up idolizing Wayne Gretzky. Drew's bedroom was adorned with Gretzky jerseys and posters, along with a Kings pillowcase and phone. Playing in Los Angeles has enabled him to meet Gretzky and another one of his heroes, David Beckham.

"Beckham is a great guy, and he was one of my favorite players growing up, so it was cool to meet him," Drew said. "He has brought so much to North American soccer, especially in Los Angeles. Gretzky made hockey in L.A., for the most part. Beckham made the Galaxy big here, too. The two have a lot in common."

While Drew is making hockey even bigger in Los Angeles, he's also helping his country continue its international dominance of the sport. He was a key part of Team Canada winning back-to-back gold medals at the Winter Olympics.

"Canada doesn't settle for anything less than a gold medal," Drew said. "When you are at the Olympics, you can feel the support miles and miles away. You know that everyone back home is watching."

To go with his two gold medals, Drew now has a pair of Stanley Cup rings after he won his second Cup with the Kings in 2014.

"Winning the Stanley Cup was one of the best moments of my life," Drew said. "I got to celebrate with my family and friends, which was amazing."

– DOUG WARD

MY FAVORITE...

Movie: *The Wolf of Wall Street*

TV Show: *Breaking Bad*

Musician: *Eric Church. I love country music*

NHL player growing up: *Wayne Gretzky*

Pre-game meal: *Pasta and alfredo sauce with chicken, shrimp and mushrooms*

Junk food: *Cinnabon*

Video game: *FIFA 14*

Sports other than hockey: *Soccer and golf*

Hockey memory: *Winning the Stanley Cup*

Way to score: *I haven't had a breakaway yet in the NHL, so my favorite would be on a breakaway, if I ever got one*

WORD SEARCH

QUICK
ROBITAILLE
GRETZKY
DOUGHTY
LOMBARDI
TAYLOR
DIONNE
SUTTER
MELROSE
BROWN
KOPITAR
CARTER
STAPLES
VACHON

S	S	N	G	R	E	T	Z	K	Y	O	W	L
A	N	O	S	N	S	O	H	I	S	T	O	A
D	C	I	H	T	O	R	S	U	T	T	E	R
R	I	T	Q	A	R	H	Z	M	G	R	V	O
E	R	O	L	N	L	P	C	N	W	O	R	B
R	P	E	N	R	E	A	U	A	T	L	B	I
A	Y	Y	C	N	M	N	U	O	V	Y	V	T
T	Y	T	J	H	E	S	F	F	U	A	R	A
I	E	H	R	R	S	E	L	P	A	T	S	I
P	T	G	T	C	A	R	T	E	R	U	C	L
O	Q	U	I	C	K	E	Z	N	S	N	O	L
K	Q	O	K	Q	L	U	O	I	N	C	N	E
V	A	D	I	D	R	A	B	M	O	L	M	Q

My First GAME

October 11, 2008
Los Angeles Kings **1**
@ San Jose Sharks **3**
1 shot, 17:40 ice time

DREW
DOUGHTY

"There's one thing about my first NHL game that I remember pretty clearly. Going into the third period, we were going on the power play. I turned to my buddy Wayne Simmonds, who was a rookie with me, and said, 'I haven't really done anything all game. I've just been playing it simple. I haven't really done anything like myself.'

"Wayne looked at me and said, 'Don't do it, don't do it.' But I went out and did it anyway. I ended up turning the puck over, which allowed the Sharks to score a goal."

CROSSWORD

ACROSS

1 Center ___ Stoll is from Saskatchewan
3 ___ MacDonald was Kings coach in the 1980s (or Spider-Man's real last name)
7 Sending the puck the length of the ice
8 A healthy ___ is a player who sits out when he's able to play
9 Was smart; ___ one's head
11 No. 1 Down missed much of 2007-08 after he ___ his ACL
14 Dean Lombardi is L.A.'s general ___
16 ___ Vachon was a legendary King, later coach and GM
17 Number worn by No. 4 Down
18 Both Jeff Carter and Drew Doughty come from this Ontario city

DOWN

1 The Kings' ___ Williams, pictured
2 Took on in a fight
4 Playmaker Anze ___ was born in Yugoslavia
5 Robyn ___ is the only Brazilian-born NHLer
6 Wayne Gretzky won three Art ___ trophies while with L.A.
10 Bench boss Darryl Sutter also coached in this California city
11 Los Angeles edged this team to go to the Cup final in 1993
12 Trophy won by Jonathan Quick in 2012
13 When the Kings joined the NHL, teams played a 74-game ___
15 Former captain Blake, and namesakes

Mascot
"Bailey"

AHL Affiliate
Manchester Monarchs

ECHL Affiliate
Ontario Reign

FAST FACTS

Captain: *Dustin Brown*

Coach: *Darryl Sutter*

GM: *Dean Lombardi*

Arena: *Staples Center*

Capacity: *18,118*

Stanley Cups: *2*

Playoff Appearances: *28*

First Season: *1967-68*

ZACH PARISE

ZACH PARISE ISN'T PERFECT. THERE ARE TIMES when you look at the star left winger and think he is. But he's not.

He's captained the New Jersey Devils and the U.S. Olympic team, has come within two victories of winning a Stanley Cup and, along with his good friend Ryan Suter, signed a 13-year, $98-million contract in 2012 to likely play the rest of his career in his home state of Minnesota.

He's a good-looking guy, as nice as can be, lives in his dream house on a lake and has a beautiful wife, wonderful parents and two healthy, cute newborn twin children. But Zach will be the first to proudly tell you it's taken a lot of hard work and even a few failures to get where he is today.

In fact, three years after his mother, Donna, introduced him to the ice, Zach was seven years old and cut from the squirt A team he was trying out for in Bloomington, Minn. His brother, Jordan, who's nearly two years older than Zach, made the team.

"That was tough," Zach said. "I did the usual 'I'm not going to play anymore, I'm quitting hockey.' But you get over it, and it makes you try harder the next time. You get back up. I'm glad I didn't quit hockey."

Zach isn't the fastest player, he isn't the most skilled, he isn't the most physical and he isn't the biggest. But he makes up for it all with an unmatched work ethic.

Come to a Wild practice and you'll see that Zach is usually the first player on the ice, tirelessly working on his shot and puckhandling. Come to a Wild game and you'll see that if the puck goes behind the net or into a corner, a relentless Zach is usually the player coming out with it. If the play is going to the front of the net, Zach is often the offensive player there, no matter the size of the defenseman he's battling with.

He learned this trait from his father, J.P. Parise, who played 13 years in the NHL and is an icon in Minnesota because of his days playing for the North Stars, who have since become the Dallas Stars.

> I LEARNED EVERYTHING FROM MY DAD – EVERYTHING ABOUT HOCKEY AND EVERYTHING ABOUT WORK ETHIC

"I learned everything from my dad – everything about hockey and everything about work ethic," Zach said. "He'd always say, 'You're not the most skilled guy, so you better work on your shot every day just to stay even with everybody else,' just to make sure I'd play."

Zach quickly learned the one thing he can always control is being the hardest worker on his team.

"And that doesn't only mean in games," J.P. said. "It means you're there, you're helping, you're the leader, you go earlier and bring kids on the ice with

you and work on deflections. That's being a worker. He took that to heart pretty good. He's humble, quiet, minds his own business, yet serious, totally dedicated and gives 100 percent to the cause. He loves to help others and is polite. I don't know where he got that from. His mother's genes are kicking in."

J.P. used to be the hockey director at Shattuck-St. Mary's, a famous prep school in Faribault, Minn., where a lot of superstar NHLers like Sidney Crosby and Nathan MacKinnon developed. That's also where Zach played his prep school hockey, scoring 146 goals and putting up 340 points in 125 games.

"I remember J.P. always calling me and saying, 'Lou, you wouldn't believe this kid. I give him keys to the rink, and he goes all night, all morning – he's just obsessed,' " said Lou Nanne, a former North Stars player, coach and general manager. "Zach just loves hockey, but he works so hard at it. That was one of J.P.'s trademarks – hard work – and it carried over to Zach."

As a two-time Hobey Baker Award finalist at the University of North Dakota, Zach became a star for the Devils but left New Jersey after going to the Stanley Cup final in 2012. Coming to Minnesota with Suter was a franchise-altering event for the Wild. It lent the team legitimacy league-wide and gave it two respected marquee stars. Plus, in a state that so loves its Minnesota-born players, Zach gives the Wild a famous born-and-bred Minnesotan.

"More than anything else, I want to win," Zach said. "You get so close last year, you want to get back there and have another crack at it. It'd even be that much more special if we can do it here. Fans here deserve a championship team."

J.P. is proud of his son, the player and the person.

"If you're going to play, you have an obligation to your team to come prepared and play to the best of

MY FAVORITE...

Movie: *Gladiator*

TV show: *Sons of Anarchy*

Musician: *George Strait*

Celebrities: *Roger Federer and Denzel Washington*

Video game: *Halo 2*

Pre-game meal: *Spaghetti and meat sauce*

Junk food: *Cookie dough*

Player growing up: *Mike Modano*

Team growing up: *Minnesota North Stars*

Sport other than hockey: *Tennis*

Hockey memory: *Going to the 2012 Stanley Cup final*

Way to score: *Empty-netter*

your ability, and you never ask him to do that because that's just the way he is," J.P. said. "He is such a good person. He's always doing stuff for young kids. Of course, it's important to be good at hockey, but that's not what's really important. He's turned out to be a real good guy." – **MICHAEL RUSSO**

WORD SEARCH

H	Q	Z	U	M	U	T	O	L	V	E	O	B
P	R	E	T	U	S	N	A	Y	R	S	P	X
O	C	F	E	G	L	E	M	A	I	R	E	C
M	D	K	E	F	O	O	L	P	S	A	C	E
I	D	I	S	L	E	F	U	Q	E	H	I	L
N	C	R	L	E	Y	L	A	U	B	I	O	E
V	H	O	E	T	E	L	P	N	R	K	R	N
I	A	B	A	C	K	S	T	R	O	M	E	E
L	R	A	V	H	I	S	I	U	R	T	R
L	D	G	Q	E	M	H	V	Z	G	C	D	G
E	I	T	H	R	R	U	T	E	H	I	Y	Y
R	N	E	S	I	R	A	P	H	C	A	Z	Y
I	G	C	I	Y	V	O	S	A	M	P	D	K

FLETCHER
HARDING
POMINVILLE
ST. PAUL
RYAN SUTER
KOIVU
MIKE YEO
LEMAIRE
BACKSTROM
GABORIK
NORDY
ZACH PARISE
RISEBROUGH
XCEL ENERGY

→ My First
GAME

October 5, 2005
Pittsburgh Penguins 1
@ New Jersey Devils 5
1 G, 1 A, 15:48 ice time

ZACH
PARISE

"I found out that I made the team and was on the opening night roster because they switched my number from 51 to 9. I was at center at the time, and I just remember I took a peek across the red line, and I saw Mario Lemieux on the ice. He was a guy that I watched and was one of my favorite players growing up. That was kind of the moment where you're just like, 'I made it.' It was pretty awesome, and I ended up scoring on my first shot and had an assist. It was cool. It was a good first game."

CROSSWORD

(Grid entries visible: "Nic" at 3 across top, "Mikko" at 16, "Star" reading down near center)

ACROSS

1 Zach ___ is a Minnesota boy
3 ___ Backstrom is from Finland
7 Be behind
8 He shares goaltending duties with No. 3 Across, pictured
9 To win ___ is to pick up points while playing poorly
11 Face
14 Mikael Granlund and Charlie Coyle are ___ with the Wild
16 Mikko ___ is another Finn
17 Parise topped American scorers when the U.S. won the ___ medal at the Olympics in Vancouver
18 Scrapped

DOWN

1 The Wild amassed a team record 104 ___ in 2006-07
2 Chuck Fletcher won a ___ Cup while working for the Penguins
4 Jacques ___ was the Wild's first coach
5 Not giving up much, like a good defense
6 First name of No. 8 Across
10 Fletcher is ___ manager
11 He's the coach
12 They search out new talent
13 Former Wild blueliner Nick Schultz was born this month
15 Minnesota hosted the 2004 All-___ Game

AHL Affiliate
Iowa
Wild

Mascot
"Nordy"

FAST FACTS

Captain: **Mikko Koivu**

Coach: **Mike Yeo**

GM: **Chuck Fletcher**

Arena: **Xcel Energy Center**

Capacity: **17,954**

Stanley Cups: **0**

Playoff Appearances: **5**

First Season: **2000-01**

P.K. SUBBAN

A LOT OF THINGS COME NATURALLY TO P.K. Subban. For starters, the guy is definitely a talker. And although that's been known to ruffle a few feathers, his bold personality is also engaging and devoid of fabrication.

But P.K.'s emergence as one of the most dynamic young defensemen in the game is owed far more to sweat than swagger, thanks to a work ethic that's easily traced to his father, Karl Subban.

"Maybe it's my teaching background," said Karl, a retired Toronto principal. "If you want to be good at something, you start young and practise frequently and good things will happen."

Karl (P.K. is Pernell Karl) immigrated to frigid Sudbury, Ont., from sunny Jamaica with his family at the age of 11. Growing up in a francophone neighborhood, Karl absorbed the love of hockey emanating from other kids on his street. His affection for the sport only grew when he began attending games of the Ontario League's Sudbury Wolves and watching the Montreal Canadiens on TV.

When it came time to start his career, Karl moved to Toronto, where he and wife, Maria, raised their five children. The girls, Nastassia and Natasha, came first, then P.K. started a trend of hockey-playing boys, with Malcolm and Jordan following. By the time he was two and a half, P.K. was on skates.

"He was still in Pampers when he started," Karl said.

P.K.'s trips with his dad to an outdoor rink in downtown Toronto as a young boy have already started to become part of Canadian hockey lore. Karl, setting the tone of hard work, was basically pulling two shifts daily, the first as an administrator, then as V-P of a continuing education program in the evening. Most people would be dreaming of a pillow instead of an ice pad after logging those hours, but Karl would walk through the door to find P.K. asleep in his snow pants.

"He'd come home and wake me up and take me down to Nathan Phillips Square," P.K. said. "I'd be skating until one or two o'clock in the morning."

Because he was young enough that he only attended school in the afternoon, P.K. was free to rest up in the morning. Karl has joked in the past that their seemingly excessive regimen wasn't child abuse, it was something they both loved to do. And for all the talk of dedication and work, Karl always found ways to reward his son.

"After every skate, he'd take me for a treat – a pizza slice or something like that," P.K. said.

Karl began making a rink in the backyard of the family home and soon, with Malcolm and Jordan

> ## PEOPLE WHO KNOW ME KNOW I'M HUMBLE. WHEN IT COMES TO PLAYING THE GAME, I'M JUST VERY COMPETITIVE

76

P.K.
SUBBAN
BORN: MAY 13, 1989
HEIGHT: 6' 0"
WEIGHT: 217 lbs
POSITION: D
SHOOTS: R

following their big brother's strides, it was a hive of activity.

"We'd be out there for hours, and I never once complained," P.K. said. "I loved to do it. I have tons of memories of those skates."

P.K.'s rise through the minor hockey ranks eventually led him to the OHL's Belleville Bulls in 2005 and then to the American League's Hamilton Bulldogs in 2009. It was during his rookie pro season of 2009-10 with the Bulldogs that P.K. made his NHL debut, a two-game February cameo with the Habs. Then, two months later, he joined the Canadiens for 14 playoff games during their run to the Eastern Conference final. Along the way, his brazen approach and theatrical celebrations prompted some members of the hockey community to suggest a rookie shouldn't carry himself in that manner.

"The people who know me know I'm humble," P.K. said. "I'm confident and I'll never back down from anybody, and I'm going to speak my mind because that's what I've been taught. But I respect the game, I respect my teammates, I respect my opponents. When it comes to playing the game, I'm just very competitive."

Of course, the reward for a job well done with the Bleu, Blanc et Rouge goes well beyond the slice of pizza P.K. used to get from his dad after their late-night skates. And if one thing can be gleaned from P.K.'s career to this point, it's that he's definitely willing to use some elbow grease in pursuit of his goals.

"I remember when he was running the hills, I used to say, 'P.K., there's a kid in Sweden, there's a kid in Russia, who's probably sleeping now and you're working hard,'" Karl said. "That was a motivating thing.

"You've got to work for what you want in life, and he's certainly learned his lessons well." – **RYAN DIXON**

MY FAVORITE...

TV show: *Scandal*

Band: *Rolling Stones*

Celebrity: *Michael Jackson. When he was alive. It would've been cool to meet him*

Video game: *I wish I played video games. Have I played one? Flappy Bird. Good game*

Pre-game meal: *Chicken, brown rice and sweet potato*

Junk food: *Sushi and red wine*

Player growing up: *Bobby Orr*

Team growing up: *Montreal Canadiens*

Sport other than hockey: *Football*

Hockey memory: *Winning the 2009 World Junior Championship in Ottawa*

Way to score: *One-timer, Game 7, Stanley Cup final, game over*

WORD SEARCH

HABS
RICHARD
BELL
PRICE
SUBBAN
BLAKE
THERRIEN
LAFLEUR
BELIVEAU
BERGEVIN
ROY
PACIORETTY
MAHOVLICH
FORUM

H	Q	Z	U	M	U	R	O	F	V	E	O	B
G	I	L	A	X	H	U	B	K	P	S	P	E
I	C	B	E	R	G	E	V	I	N	K	A	P
L	R	F	V	A	A	L	C	P	B	A	C	L
S	I	L	I	K	E	F	H	Q	E	H	I	C
O	C	E	L	Y	O	A	X	U	E	I	O	V
H	H	S	E	R	F	L	T	P	K	R	R	O
N	A	B	B	U	S	D	L	J	A	N	E	D
M	R	T	V	A	U	V	Z	E	L	E	T	E
Z	D	Z	Q	I	H	H	X	Z	B	C	T	U
Y	T	T	H	E	R	R	I	E	N	I	Y	T
R	V	I	W	P	X	V	K	P	E	R	O	Y
I	H	C	I	L	V	O	H	A	M	P	D	K

My First
GAME

February 12, 2010
Montreal Canadiens **2**
@ Philadelphia Flyers **3**
1 A, 18:04 ice time

P.K.
SUBBAN

"First NHL game was against Philadelphia, in Philly. It was pretty cool. It ended up being a loss, and we played them back-to-back. We played them that day, and then we played the next day against Philly as well. I had an assist in the game. I remember I got into it with Chris Pronger, and he told me my breath stank. That's pretty funny."

CROSSWORD

ACROSS

1 Brian ___ was captain in Montreal
3 P.K. ___ was the latest Hab to win the Norris Trophy
7 Rick ___ was the first-overall pick in 1976 and won a Cup with Montreal a decade later
8 A team that's trailing late may ___ its bench
9 Threesome, like a forward line
11 Travis ___, pictured, is on the wing
14 Guy ___ thrilled Habs fans back in the 1970s
16 Defeat unexpectedly
17 Number worn by Brendan Gallagher
18 The Habs play at the Bell ___

DOWN

1 ___ Hainsworth was a legendary netminder with Montreal
2 Montreal's longtime rival, both are Original Six teams
4 Easily injured
5 Saku Koivu led all scorers when the Winter Olympics were held here in 1998
6 The Habs have won a whopping 24 Stanley ___
10 One who wears a striped shirt
11 The Rocket's first name
12 Jacques ___ revolutionized the game by wearing a mask
13 As a player ages, he may lose a ___ or two
15 ___ Walter played for Montreal from 1982 to 1991

Mascot
"Youppi!"

AHL Affiliate
Hamilton Bulldogs

ECHL Affiliate
Wheeling Nailers

FAST FACTS

Captain: *Vacant*

Coach: *Michel Therrien*

GM: *Marc Bergevin*

Arena: *Bell Centre*

Capacity: *21,273*

Stanley Cups: *24*

Playoff Apperances: *81*

First Season: *1917-18*

PEKKA **RINNE**

BY DEFINITION, DREAMS ARE A FARSIGHTED proposition. They require one to look off into the distance, beyond reality and into possibility. They're not always in focus, which sometimes provides the dreamer with more of a general direction than an actual destination. The risk, of course, is that they'll vanish before they become real.

When gazing off into the landscape of dreams, though, there often are so many possibilities it can be difficult to know where to look. That's often been the case for Pekka Rinne.

As a teenager in Kempele, Finland, it was tough for him to imagine things could get much better than to be goalie on a tier II junior team that included a lot of his friends. They played together during the winters and then moved on to baseball or soccer in the summers. It seemed a reasonable goal to aspire to one day play for his favorite team, Karpat, a mere 15 minutes away in Oulu, which was a competitive, though not a dominant, team. Everything Pekka thought he wanted was right there in front of him.

Then his coach at the time opened his mind's eye to a world of possibilities, a world in which Pekka not only tested himself daily against the best hockey players, but where he was one of the best – a two-

> ## I DIDN'T HAVE A CLUE ABOUT GETTING DRAFTED. A LOT OF FINNISH PLAYERS GET DRAFTED AND NOT A LOT HAPPENS

time Vezina Trophy finalist before his 30th birthday and good enough that a franchise now builds its entire team around his abilities. Jarri Jautamaki was one of the first who told Pekka to dream bigger.

"He thought I was too good to play at that level and thought I needed to start training more and pushing myself to go to a better team and a top level in junior hockey," Pekka said. "It took me a while to understand that, but it wasn't long after that my whole mindset and workload and everything changed."

Pekka focused on hockey year-round. He got on with Karpat's junior team and made the pro/senior roster as a 20-year-old in 2003-04. He played 14 games and helped the team to a championship. It seemed all that was left to accomplish was to become the No. 1 goalie, a title that belonged to Niklas Backstrom, who now plays goal for the Minnesota Wild.

Then once again somebody showed him a different dream. The Nashville Predators selected Pekka in the eighth round (258th overall) of the 2004 draft, and before long then-assistant general manager Ray Shero and then-goalie coach Mitch Korn paid him a visit to discuss the possibilities they envisioned for him.

"I didn't really have a clue about getting drafted,"

35

PEKKA RINNE

BORN: NOV. 3, 1982
HEIGHT: 6' 5"
WEIGHT: 204 lbs
POSITION: G
SHOOTS: L

Pekka said. "I was at a big summer party at a cottage with my buddies when I got the call. I was proud of it, and it meant a lot. At the same time I didn't really make anything of it. I thought it was cool. A lot of Finnish players get drafted and not a lot happens."

He participated in Nashville's prospects conditioning camp that summer and finally saw all the possibilities. Once he did, things happened quickly.

A year later he accepted the organization's contract offer, became the top goalie for the Milwaukee Admirals of the American League and led them to the 2006 Calder Cup final. He graduated to a full-time NHL goalie in 2008-09 and early that season became Nashville's No. 1, a spot that's been his ever since and will remain so jduging by the seven-year, $49-million deal he signed in November 2012.

It hasn't always been easy. He missed much of 2006-07 because of a shoulder injury sustained in a freak, off-ice incident during the off-season. And an infection in his hip sidelined him for nearly five months of 2013-14 and threatened his career.

Through it all, Pekka has never lost focus. Not when so many others, like Jautamaki or Finnish goalie coach Ari Hilli or Predators scouts and executives, all saw the same thing and consistently pointed him in the same direction. He's achieved so much and gone so far that he's reached a point where it's now a joy to look back occasionally.

Late in 2013-14, for example, Jautamaki visited Pekka in the United States for the first time. They reminisced as they walked around the Predators' home, Bridgestone Arena, with its pristine dressing room, expansive weight room and all the other first-class amenities around every corner and behind every door. It looked nothing like the rink where they had come together in Kempele, which wasn't much of a rink at all. It was an ice surface covered by an air

MY FAVORITE...

TV show: *Californication*

Musician: *Neil Young*

Actor: *Leonardo DiCaprio*

Junk food: *Chocolate*

Way to relax: *Watching a movie*

Vacation spot: *Italy*

Off-day activity: *Fishing*

School subject: *Geography*

Sport other than hockey: *Soccer or tennis*

vacuum bubble with barracks for a dressing room.

"He was actually pretty emotional at how things have changed and how far I've come," Pekka said.

In a way, though, he'd already seen it all years ago.

— DAVID BOCLAIR

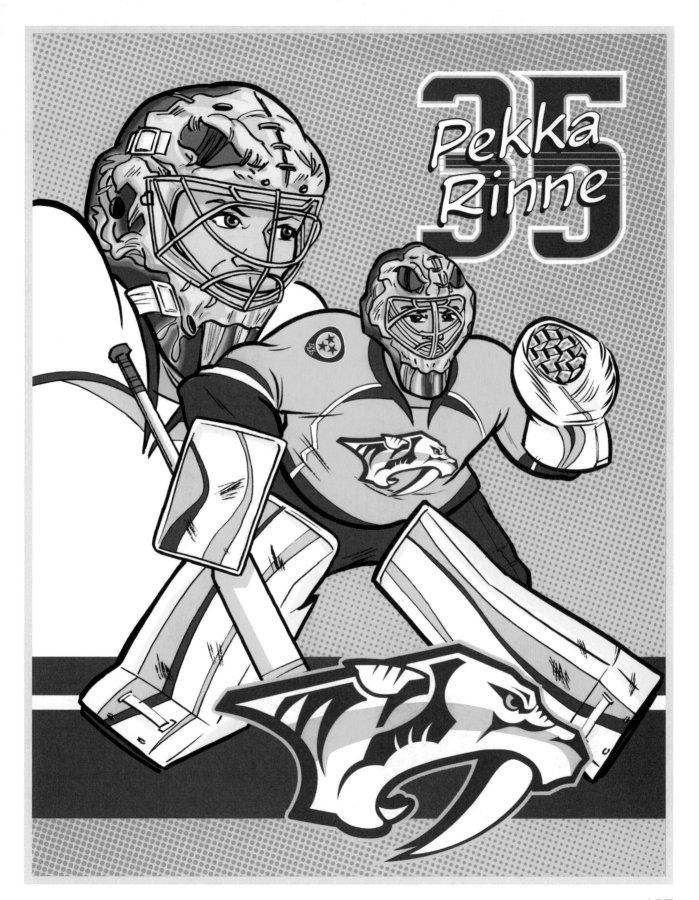

WORD SEARCH

CRAIG SMITH
HUTTON
BARRY TROTZ
TOOTOO
SHEA WEBER
FISHER
SETH JONES
GNASH
HORNQVIST
BRIDGESTONE
MUSIC CITY
POILE
PEKKA RINNE
LEGWAND

B	N	S	T	S	I	V	Q	N	R	O	H	H
Y	Y	T	R	I	L	K	L	E	S	L	P	C
V	T	S	E	N	O	J	H	T	E	S	E	S
C	I	G	N	L	E	G	W	A	N	D	K	H
R	C	Z	O	E	N	A	K	W	A	I	K	U
A	C	U	T	A	G	V	A	N	H	X	A	T
I	I	Y	S	N	O	O	T	O	O	T	R	T
G	S	H	E	A	W	E	B	E	R	J	I	O
S	U	X	G	F	I	S	H	E	R	A	N	N
M	M	U	D	U	S	T	N	L	W	I	N	B
I	P	V	I	D	K	N	E	I	S	H	E	U
T	B	A	R	R	Y	T	R	O	T	Z	N	D
H	A	T	B	L	O	W	O	P	T	E	M	H

→My First GAME

December 15, 2005
*Chicago Blackhawks **3**
@ Nashville Predators **5**
Win, 35 saves, .921 SP*

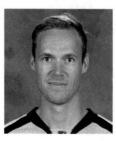

PEKKA
RINNE

"Everything happened so quickly. I was playing in the minors with Brian Finley and was really good buddies with him. Nashville's goalies Tomas Vokoun and Chris Mason were both hurt. Brian Finley played the night before in Florida and the team lost. Right after that game they called me up. I was pretty nervous. I remember I had quite a bit of work. Then I remember being named one of the game's stars. I really didn't think that way. I thought they were just being nice to me."

CROSSWORD

ACROSS

1 Mike ___ is an alternate captain
3 Swedish-born ___ Stalberg, pictured, is on the wing
7 Rich ___ is also a winger with Nashville
8 Former Predator Kimmo ___ was captain for a season
9 Beat unexpectedly; knock unconscious
11 Cubicle
14 Gabriel ___ is from Rimouski in Quebec
16 Craig ___ hails from Wisconsin, a hockey hotbed
17 Block the view of the goalie
18 No Predator has won the Conn ___ Trophy

DOWN

1 Being from Quebec, No. 14 Across also speaks this language
2 You'd think the Predators would be in the ___ Conference, but they're not
4 Where No. 7 Across hails from
5 Ranking
6 At center is ___ Cullen
10 Goalie Carter Hutton is from ___ Bay, Ont.
11 This American-born Predator is from New York State
12 Occupy all one's thoughts
13 A ___ is a scoring opportunity
15 First name of No. 11 Down

Mascot
"Gnash"

AHL Affiliate
Milwaukee Admirals

ECHL Affiliate
Cincinnati Cyclones

FAST FACTS

Captain: **Shea Weber**

Coach: **Peter Laviolette**

GM: **David Poile**

Arena: **Bridgestone Arena**

Capacity: **17,113**

Stanley Cups: **0**

Playoff Appearances: **7**

First Season: **1998-99**

DEVILS

CORY SCHNEIDER

CORY SCHNEIDER'S PARENTS STILL HAVE THE T-shirt their son designed as a nine-year-old with dreams of playing in the NHL. It was an art project in fourth grade, and there was never any doubt about what he wanted to say.

"You had to make a T-shirt and write your name on it," Cory said. "It says: 'Hi, my name is Cory. I have an older brother. When I grow up I want to be an NHL goalie.' I don't think I actually knew back then, but that's the first recorded evidence we have of that."

He laughs about it today, but Cory admits he didn't truly believe until much later that his dream would come true.

"When did I think I had a chance to become an NHL player? Probably not until my first training camp," he said with a chuckle. "I don't know if there is ever actually a time when you say, 'This is what I'm going to do.' It just kind of evolves and happens. As you realize it's a possibility, you just keep pushing toward that goal."

Growing up in Marblehead, Mass., Cory played soccer and baseball as well as hockey. He remains an avid Boston Red Sox fan. His baseball position?

"Catcher, obviously," he said. "I just enjoy wearing the equipment, to stand out from everybody else. I played baseball all the way through high school and only stopped when I got to college. I wish I could've dedicated some more time to it, but my summers were spent playing hockey."

While Cory showed promise as a goalie, his true potential didn't become obvious until prep school at Phillips Academy in Andover, Mass.

"He came to Andover as a sophomore," said Dean Boylan, who coached Cory on the Phillips Academy Big Blue. "He came in certainly as a very raw goaltender, but he was extremely competitive from the get-go. He had to adjust to the speed and skill level, but he did that.

"Some of his early games probably weren't his best. But, boy, halfway through the year, Cory was starting to really get it and play extremely well. We started to see we had something very special. Did we ever envision a No. 1 draft pick in the NHL? No, I can't say that we did, but we knew we had something very special with him."

It was at Boston College, under coach Jerry York, that Cory began to get noticed.

"A lot has been said about him, but it's all true," Cory said of his college coach. "What a good role model he is. In terms of coming to college, at 18 you're looking to have fun and enjoy your time. He helps you head in the right direction, mature, be-

> **I'VE JUST ALWAYS FELT THAT EVERY TIME I STEP ON THE ICE I HAVE TO PROVE THAT I BELONG HERE**

come an adult, learn discipline and responsibility."

Cory needed that foundation, along with constant encouragement from his dad, Rich, and mom, Sue, to take the next step.

The Vancouver Canucks selected Cory 26th overall in the 2004 draft, but his first pro season was rocky. He shared the net for the Manitoba Moose of the American League, but lost the No. 1 job to Drew MacIntyre. At that point, he questioned whether he was NHL material.

"The first half of the season was pretty abysmal for me," Cory said. "It didn't go very well. I came in thinking I knew everything about the pro game and didn't have to change what I was doing. I had to get set straight a little bit."

Scott Arniel was the Manitoba coach.

"He was actually the one who called me in and said, 'Look, you obviously have talent but you have to work harder and be more dedicated,'" Cory said. "He wasn't as kind as that, but that was basically the gist of it. He really sort of gave me an ultimatum and made me aware of the situation. Pretty much after that meeting it turned around and went in the right direction."

Cory feels fortunate to have overcame the adversity, and on Nov. 29, 2008, he made his NHL debut for the Canucks.

"It wasn't that I was lazy or wasn't trying," he said. "You just have to learn how to be a pro. It's your job now. It's not just an after-school activity or in college where you still have to go to class. It's what you do. I was lucky that the team and the organization were patient with me and let me work it out."

Cory left Boston College after his third year and made a deal with his father that he'd complete college. It took him three summers of classes to earn his degree in finance.

MY FAVORITE...

TV show: *Wired*

Celebrity: *Will Ferrell*

Band: *Green Day*

Pre-game meal: *Chicken*

Junk food: *Ice cream. When I can have it*

Player growing up: *Mike Richter*

Team growing up: *Boston Bruins*

After sharing goaltending duties in Vancouver with Roberto Luongo, he was traded to New Jersey June 30, 2013, where he played alongside Martin Brodeur in his first season with the Devils.

"The thought is to constantly prove that you belong, and that you're as good as everyone thinks you are, because goaltending is a funny position," Cory said. "You can be on top of the world one day, and the next day you wonder if you have any talent. I've just always felt that every time I step on the ice I need to prove I belong here and that I can do this. The minute you start thinking that you've got it figured out, that you're better than everybody else, you run into some problems."

Sounds like a message for a T-shirt. **– RICH CHERE**

Cory Schneider
30

WORD SEARCH

SALVADOR
ZAJAC
ELIAS
JAROMIR
LAMORIELLO
DEBOER
PRUDENTIAL
NEWARK
LEMAIRE
SCHNEIDER
STANLEY CUP
STEVENS
HENRIQUE
BRODEUR

B	R	G	Z	S	T	E	V	E	N	S	S	H
Y	D	N	L	A	I	T	N	E	D	U	R	P
V	L	E	F	D	J	E	C	K	U	A	M	S
R	J	W	Y	I	S	A	E	R	L	W	L	A
S	T	A	N	L	E	Y	C	U	P	I	A	L
C	B	R	R	L	K	B	T	E	E	F	M	V
H	R	K	I	O	M	N	L	D	L	I	O	A
N	E	A	H	S	M	H	P	O	E	K	R	D
E	S	E	O	N	T	I	V	R	M	P	I	O
I	N	D	E	B	O	E	R	B	A	P	E	R
D	U	Y	V	I	J	S	T	L	I	U	L	D
E	J	I	T	U	E	D	N	E	R	L	L	Y
R	T	O	E	U	Q	I	R	N	E	H	O	R

→ *My First*
GAME

November 28, 2008
Vancouver Canucks 1
@ Calgary Flames 3
28 saves, .903 SP

CORY
SCHNEIDER

"*Roberto Luongo pulled his groin, so the Canucks called me up from Manitoba. I remember my first game was as a backup against Detroit. A couple of games later, we were in Calgary. We were finishing the morning skate, and coach (Alain) Vigneault came up to me and said, 'You're in tonight.' So that's as much of a warning as I got. They probably did it on purpose so I wouldn't be too nervous. It was a loss, but I made some saves. I stopped (Jarome) Iginla and a few guys, so I thought, 'Maybe I can do this.'*"

CROSSWORD

ACROSS

1 Peter ___ is behind the bench
3 Puts the biscuit in the basket, like Patrik Elias does a lot
7 Number retired by the Devils (or the number of Stanley Cups they have won)
8 Jacques ___ was coach when the Devils won their first Cup
9 An old arena is known as a ___
11 This veteran Czech winger continues to rack up the points in Jersey, pictured
14 Eric ___ is a blueliner with New Jersey
16 Tuomo ___ was a late-season pick-up
17 Playoffs are best-of-seven ___
18 ___ Zajac is a Winnipeg boy

DOWN

1 First appearances
2 The Devils belong to the NHL's ___ Conference
4 Controlling the puck by clever stickhandling
5 Brent ___ was behind the bench in Jersey for a couple seasons
6 Cory Schneider is now the starter in ___ in New Jersey
10 Martin Brodeur has played in nine NHL ___-___ Games
11 First name of No. 11 Across
12 Michael Ryder and No. 11 Across were acquired by the Devils as free ___
13 Dainius ___ is on the wing
15 The Devils were just the conference's fifth ___ when they won their first Cup

Mascot
"NJ Devil"

AHL Affiliate
Albany Devils

FAST FACTS

Captain: *Bryce Salvador*

Coach: *Peter DeBoer*

GM: *Lou Lamoriello*

Arena: *Prudential Center*

Capacity: *17,625*

Stanley Cups: *3*

Playoff Appearances: *22*

First Season: *1974-75*

KYLE OKPOSO

YOU MIGHT THINK A YOUNG MAN WITH THE type of talent Kyle Okposo possesses had a clear and easy route to NHL glory. If you did, you'd be dead wrong. Despite being blessed with incredible on-ice tools, Kyle has faced and overcome numerous challenges on the road to building a successful professional hockey career. And those challenges didn't end when the New York Islanders selected him with the seventh-overall pick in the 2006 draft. That's when the journey really got tough.

Kyle first encountered serious challenges to his development in his second year of college hockey at the University of Minnesota. He'd had a banner rookie season (19 goals and 40 points in 40 games) after leaving the Shattuck-St. Mary's hockey factory boarding school, but his sophomore season didn't bring the same success. He had a strong first game of the season but went nine games without a point and wasn't getting opportunities.

"That was a low point," Kyle said. "I had a lot of mental doubts, and that's not a good way to play. But I had a meeting with Tom Ward, a coach of mine at Shattuck, and that helped."

In what was one of the most difficult decisions of his life, Kyle chose to turn pro in December of that sophomore collegiate season and spent the spring of 2008 in the American League with the Islanders' affiliate in Bridgeport, Conn. Kyle got his feet wet with 35 AHL games and a nine-game stint with the Islanders before making the permanent jump to the NHL in 2008-09, in which he put up 18 goals and 39 points as a rookie. He did even better in his second season, with 19 goals and 52 points in 80 games. Things looked great.

Like most young players, however, he soon had to deal with his share of challenges. A shoulder injury cost him 44 games in 2010-11, and after setting a career high in goals (24) in 2011-12, things fell apart for him in 2012-13 when he managed just four goals and 24 points. This was the lowest point of his NHL career, a point when he questioned everything and was on the brink of despair.

"That season, I was really struggling, wasn't playing well and my game was lost," Kyle said. "I was stuck between being a skilled guy, a power forward and a grinder. It was a really difficult stretch for me."

So despite being just 24 years old at the time, he embarked on a reboot of his career. He began working with renowned skills coach Darryl Belfry to break down his game and rebuild it stronger than it had been before. In Kyle, Belfry saw someone who had

> THAT WAS A LOW POINT. I HAD A LOT OF MENTAL DOUBTS, AND THAT'S NOT A GOOD WAY TO PLAY

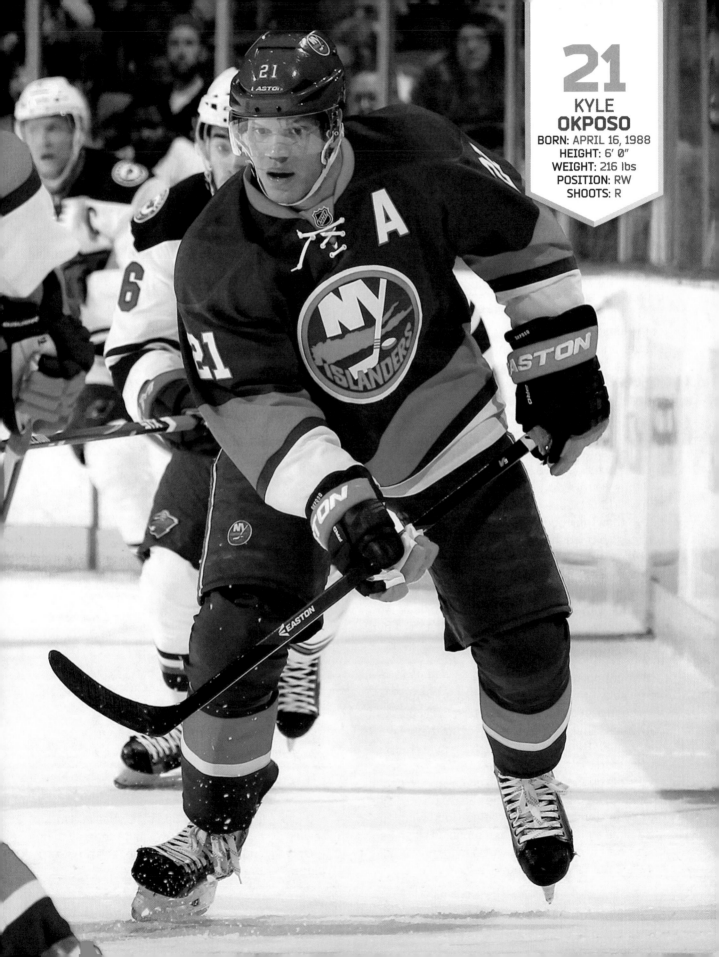

experienced a problem that affects many elite young players: he couldn't figure out what was preventing him from doing well. He'd been spoken to largely in clichés and needed an outside perspective.

"His game needed a lot of work," Belfry said. "One of the issues he had was he wasn't using his best assets, and his confidence base took a major hit because of that. He became disconnected from the habits that were going to make him successful in the NHL. Sometimes the player is the last to know how good he could be, and Kyle was one of those guys."

Belfry calls Kyle a "physical freak" and one of the top two or three athletes he's ever worked with. But as far as Belfry was concerned, that wasn't the issue with him. Most elite young players are so much better than their peers until they get to the world's top league. Once they're there, that changes for everyone (except Sidney Crosby). At that point, it's how they apply their skill set and, most importantly, their mindset that makes the most difference. So while Belfry could work with him on specific areas, and he did (Kyle's shot became much better under his tutelage), it was the mental side of the game that needed the most adjusting.

"The change in his mindset was a complete 180," Belfry said. "We told Kyle, 'You can dominate if you take control of the space and determine your own outcomes.' That creates a sense of certainty and confidence. That's what we saw from Kyle once he understood that."

With his confidence restored, Kyle set new career bests in 2013-14, with 27 goals and 69 points in 72 games, and was primed to continue improving. His life gained a different, deeper dimension when he became a father in 2014, but he's more prepared to handle any challenges that will arise.

MY FAVORITE...

Movie: *The Count of Monte Cristo*

TV show: *Homeland*

Musicians: *Eminem, and I really like Luke Bryan*

Celebrity: *Denzel Washington*

Sports celebrity: *Tiger Woods, Michael Jordan*

Video game: *Call of Duty*

Pre-game meal: *Brown rice pasta and meat sauce*

Junk food: *Cinnabon*

Player growing up: *Joe Sakic*

Team growing up: *Colorado*

Sport other than hockey: *Golf*

Golf course: *Jupiter Hills in Florida*

Hockey memory: *Winning a national championship in junior for Des Moines, and also at Shattuck*

Way to score: *Top shelf*

"I give a lot of credit to Darryl," Kyle said. "I'm feeling confident and positive about the way things are going, and I just want to continue to grow as a player." – ADAM PROTEAU

WORD SEARCH

CAPUANO
TAVARES
NASSAU
DYNASTY
NIELSEN
POTVIN
CLUTTERBUCK
OKPOSO
AL ARBOUR
BILL TORREY
TROTTIER
BILLY SMITH
BOSSY
GARTH SNOW

H	S	N	T	R	O	T	T	I	E	R	O	N
P	C	A	P	U	A	N	O	Y	A	S	I	E
O	L	J	S	E	R	A	V	A	T	V	E	P
R	U	I	E	M	U	B	O	P	T	N	H	L
I	T	K	S	L	O	F	K	O	D	I	T	Q
N	T	E	L	T	B	T	P	U	N	E	I	E
G	E	V	S	T	R	L	O	N	R	L	M	U
I	R	M	A	N	A	S	S	A	U	S	S	G
L	B	B	I	L	L	T	O	R	R	E	Y	R
X	U	Y	T	S	A	N	Y	D	G	N	L	O
E	C	T	H	R	R	U	T	E	H	I	L	D
R	K	E	B	O	S	S	Y	H	C	A	I	Y
I	W	O	N	S	H	T	R	A	G	P	B	K

My First GAME

MARCH 18, 2008
Toronto Maple Leafs **3**
@ New York Islanders **1**
2 shots, 14:45 ice time

KYLE
OKPOSO

"I don't remember the whole day, but I remember being extremely nervous. I hadn't practised with the team, so I went to the rink, but didn't know what to expect. I played with Blake Comeau and Richard Park for most of the game. We lost, but I remember Rob Davidson scoring a goal from our own end on (Toronto goalie) Vesa Toskala. Right after Rob scored, (then-Islanders coach) Ted Nolan turned to me and said, 'See how easy it is to score in this league, kid?' I got a kick out of that."

CROSSWORD

ACROSS

1 ___ Nabokov played for the Islanders from 2011 to 2014
3 Kyle Okposo hails from this Minnesota city
7 Is on the receiving end of a check; ___ a hit
8 One who begins a game
9 ___ Tavares or ex-Isle Tonelli
11 Hometown of No. 15 Down (or a kind of fish)
14 Showy or impressive, like Tavares
16 Pre-game meal choice
17 Hold firmly, like a top defenseman is said to do
18 Bill ___ was Islanders GM from 1972 to 1992

DOWN

1 NHL teams played this many games when the Islanders won their first of four Cups
2 Frans ___ is from Denmark
4 The Islanders last hosted the ___-___ Game in 1983
5 The Isles have been ___ just once in five Cup final appearances
6 GM Garth Snow was once in the ___ at Nassau Coliseum
10 Tavares and Michael Grabner took part in the 2014 ___ Games in Sochi
11 Jack ___ is coach on Long Island
12 Where Tavares played his junior hockey
13 Josh ___, pictured, is a lesser-known Islander
15 Calvin de ___ is an Isles prospect (12th overall in 2009)

Mascot
"Sparky the Dragon"

AHL Affiliate
Bridgeport Sound Tigers

ECHL Affiliate
Stockton Thunder

FAST FACTS

Captain: *John Tavares*

Coach: *Jack Capuano*

GM: *Garth Snow*

Arena: *Nassau Coliseum*

Capacity: *16,170*

Stanley Cups: *4*

Playoff Appearances: *22*

First Season: *1972-73*

MARTIN ST-LOUIS

GAINING DECENT ACCESS TO THE ATHLETES during the Stanley Cup final is a little like herding cats, which is to say it's impossible. So in recent years, the NHL has adopted its own version of media day on the eve of the final. It's similar to Super Bowl media day, minus the thousands of creepy fans watching, the corporate sponsors and the marriage proposals.

With more than 1,300 accredited media for the 2014 final, however, there were a lot of questions. Players sat at individual podiums, wearing snappy polo shirts with their numbers embossed over their right breasts, and repeatedly answered them with nary a thought of going postal.

Naturally, a group gravitated toward Martin St-Louis. From his unlikely NHL career to his trade demand to his family tragedy to his playoff heroics, there was a lot of grist for the mill.

Over the past 16 years, Martin has gone from an undersized afterthought to the final laps of what will likely be a Hall of Fame career by being two things: fast and slick. These qualities were passed on to him by his father, Normand, who was known for his quickness and apparently had some pretty good moves himself. Take the day he laid eyes on France Theroux, for example. He met her at a party on a Sunday in Montreal and his heart stood still. From that moment on, it was a full-court press.

"I was with my brother and he said to me, 'Whoa, there,' and I said, 'No, that's the girl who is going to be my wife,' " Normand recalled. "I met her on Jan. 3 and I asked her to marry me on Jan. 10, one week later. I always said it was the best contract I ever signed. She put up with me for 43 years."

They were married June 26, 1971, and would have celebrated their 43rd wedding anniversary in the spring of 2014 not long after their son's 39th birthday and the Stanley Cup final. But on the afternoon of May 8, France was having a bowl of soup for lunch at the kitchen table with Normand when she noticed a pain on the right side of her chest. Since it didn't seem to be near her heart, neither she nor her husband gave it much thought. But when France awoke from a nap later that day clearly in distress, Normand called 9-1-1. France went into surgery almost immediately after arriving at the hospital, but doctors couldn't remove the blockage in her aorta. She died on the operating table. She was 63.

When Martin's mother passed, the Rangers were down 3-1 to the Pittsburgh Penguins and had just come off their worst performance of the playoffs.

> MY MOM WOULD JUST LOOK ME STRAIGHT IN THE EYES AND TELL ME TO CHASE MY DREAM

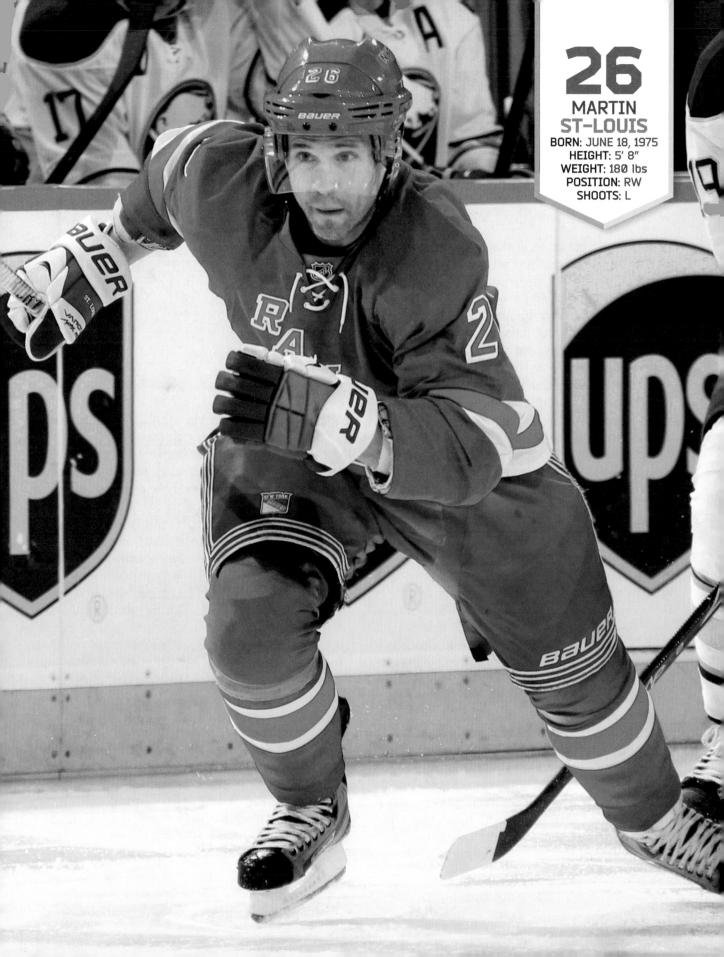

"We had put ourselves in a really tough spot, and we didn't think things could get any worse," said Henrik Lundqvist. "Then we found out that things can actually get a lot worse."

Without trivializing a moment so devastating, Martin continued to play, and the way the Rangers rallied around him provided a seminal moment in the playoffs. By the time France was buried 10 days later, the Rangers had vanquished the Penguins and were ahead of the Montreal Canadiens 1-0 en route to the Eastern Conference championship. It's impossible to know how Martin and the Rangers would have responded if they hadn't endured what they did, but there's little doubt for Martin and Normand that France remained very much an inspiration for her son.

"He is not skating alone," Normand said. "He has an angel with him. She is my angel and she is always going to be our angel."

On media day, Martin was prepared for the questions he faced. Most players pay homage to their fathers, and there's no doubt Normand had a lot to do with his son's success. One of 14 children, Normand worked at the family lumber mill before becoming a letter carrier in Laval, Que. To make extra money to send his children to private school and to help pay for his son's hockey, he built four homes from the ground up. One of them was on rue des Petunias, where Martin grew up. As a teenager, Martin helped his father in construction, but clearly he had a calling to something that wasn't manual labor.

That was hockey. Yet Martin's struggles to make it in the game are well documented. He was always the smallest player on the team, and whenever he would question himself, his mother would be there to tell him one thing: "Poursuis tes rêves." Chase your dreams.

"Since she passed, you start to think a little bit about how she shaped you," Martin said. "A lot of my work ethic, I got that from my dad, but the more I think about it this past month or so, my mom's determination...as a kid she would always tell me in French to chase my dreams. She was always really intense when she would tell me. This is a 4-foot-11 lady who would just look at me straight in my eyes and tell me to chase my dream. And show them, show them."

For the better part of two decades, Martin has been doing just that. Every time he was waived through the NHL and cut without a thought from a training camp, he would remember those words his mother told him while intently staring into his eyes.

"She was a great lady," he says. "Probably the best human being I'll ever know."

For 34 years, France worked on the assembly line at a drug company in Laval. Eight years ago, she and Normand retired and spent much of their time travelling around North America in a motor home. Things will be different for Normand, for Martin's sister, Isabelle, and for Martin himself.

"Marty is going to miss her, he's missing her a lot right now," Normand said. "He's thinking of his mother often." **– KEN CAMPBELL**

WORD SEARCH

PATRICK
LEETCH
MOORE
DAN BOYLE
HOWELL
MARC STAAL
GLEN SATHER
MESSIER
VIGNEAULT
ST. LOUIS
MADISON
GILBERT
LUNDQVIST
MCDONAGH

D	Q	R	E	H	T	A	S	N	E	L	G	B
R	D	I	Y	V	R	A	N	O	E	E	S	K
L	C	D	E	I	E	K	C	I	R	T	A	P
A	R	F	I	G	B	Y	Q	O	B	A	N	L
A	S	A	L	N	L	O	O	S	D	A	L	E
T	M	P	R	E	I	M	F	I	E	E	N	L
S	C	D	U	A	G	T	R	U	W	M	O	Y
C	D	S	M	U	S	P	H	O	W	J	S	O
R	O	L	V	L	U	C	H	L	L	E	I	B
A	N	U	Q	T	T	H	C	T	B	C	D	N
M	A	N	H	E	R	T	I	S	N	I	A	A
S	G	R	E	I	S	S	E	M	K	T	M	D
I	H	L	U	N	D	Q	V	I	S	T	S	S

My First
GAME

October 9, 1998
San Jose Sharks 3
@ Calgary Flames 3
2 shots

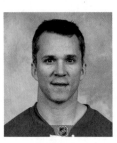

MARTIN
ST-LOUIS

Calgary
(1998-2000)

Tampa Bay
(2000-2014)

NY Rangers
(2014-present)

First NHL
Goal ('98)

Stanley Cup ('04)
Hart Memorial Trophy ('04)
Art Ross Trophy ('04,'12)
Lady Byng Trophy ('10,'11,'12)

CROSSWORD

ACROSS

1 Derek ___ is a top playmaker with the Rangers
3 Glen ___ is GM
7 Alain Vigneault won the Jack ___ Award (as NHL coach of the year) in 2007
8 The Rangers last won the ___ Cup in 1994, when Mike Keenan was coach
9 Refs in baseball
11 A team's top scorers are known as its big ___
14 Finishes
16 Martin St-Louis plays ___ wing
17 ___ Lundqvist, pictured, is between the pipes in New York
18 Former Rangers coach ___ Bergeron was known as 'The Little Tiger'

DOWN

1 The Rangers once had a 14-game home winning ___
2 No. 12 Down racked up 741 ___ to set the team mark
4 Carl ___ is a Swedish-born Ranger
5 Passes
6 ___ Zuccarello is from Oslo, Norway
10 The Rangers play at ___ Square Garden
11 Dan ___ is an alternate captain in New York
12 Brian ___ succeeded Mark Messier as captain
13 Ryan McDonagh is from this Minnesota city (it's also the home of the Wild)
15 New York last hosted the All-___ Game in 1994

AHL Affiliate
Hartford Wolf Pack

ECHL Affiliate
Greenville Road Warriors

FAST FACTS

Captain: *Vacant*

Coach: *Alain Vigneault*

GM: *Glen Sather*

Arena: *Madison Square Garden*

Capacity: *18,200*

Stanley Cups: *4*

Playoff Appearances: *56*

First Season: *1926-27*

KYLE **TURRIS**

WHEN THE OTTAWA SENATORS ACQUIRED KYLE Turris from the Coyotes for prospect David Rundblad and a second-round draft pick in December 2011, the club was hoping he was a late bloomer. And after he completed his third season in Ottawa, Senators fans are reaping the benefits.

Kyle set career highs in goals (26), assists (32) and points (58) in 2013-14. Linemate Clarke MacArthur, the prime beneficiary of Kyle's playmaking abilities, set a career high himself with 24 goals. Whether it was killing penalties, centering the power play or playing with the game on the line, Kyle was a go-to player for coach Paul MacLean. He topped all Senators forwards in average ice time at 18:43 per game.

> COMING TO THE OTTAWA SENATORS WAS LIKE A SECOND CHANCE. I WAS SO THANKFUL TO GET IT

With former captain Jason Spezza missing almost all of 2012-13 due to back surgery, Kyle was thrust into the No. 1 center role. Although he admitted it was tough at times, the low-key Kyle appreciated the opportunity.

"I can't thank coach MacLean, (general manager) Bryan Murray and the guys in the room enough to have the confidence in me," he said. "I feel like I did an OK job. At times I struggled, I had ups and downs, like a learning curve. I tried to get better every day and take things I learned last year into this year."

Murray recognized that Kyle was ready to make the next step and rewarded him with a five-year contract extension at season's end.

As a teen, Kyle appeared destined to become a professional athlete. While attending St. Thomas More Collegiate in New Westminster, B.C., he excelled in football, golf and lacrosse, the last of which runs in the family. His dad, Bruce, is a member of the Canadian Lacrosse Hall of Fame. It's no surprise, then, that Kyle was a star lacrosse player for the junior New Westminster Salmonbellies. Hockey, however, is where Kyle found the most success.

He amassed 193 points in 110 games playing two seasons for the Burnaby Express of the British Columbia League. The club won the Royal Bank Cup in his first campaign, and Kyle led the Jr. A loop with 66 goals in his second. This is when Kyle first caught the eyes of NHL scouts. The NHL Central Scouting Bureau ranked him No. 1 among North American skaters in advance of the 2007 draft.

The 2007-08 season was a whirlwind for Kyle. It started off in June with him being selected third overall by the Coyotes in the draft. Then, he enrolled at the University of Wisconsin. He followed that up by claiming gold at the '08 world juniors, compiling

7

KYLE
TURRIS
BORN: AUG. 14, 1989
HEIGHT: 6' 1"
WEIGHT: 191 lbs
POSITION: C
SHOOTS: R

a team-leading eight points in the process. And, finally, he made his NHL debut.

Hockey experts questioned Kyle's decision to attend Wisconsin rather than join the Western League's Vancouver Giants, who held his junior rights, but Kyle set the record straight.

"I was a really small kid," he said. "I didn't start growing until Grade 11-12. I just felt that the university route would give me four years, if needed, to physically develop and grow. At the same time, getting an education was important as well. Going into the draft, I told all them teams I would come out if asked. That's why I left university. I loved Wisconsin. That's part of my life that I cherish."

Kyle was looking forward to his rookie season, especially playing under coach Wayne Gretzky. Unfortunately, he was hampered by a lingering back injury. Fearing possible nerve damage, he underwent emergency surgery to repair a herniated disc.

The 2010-11 season may have been the biggest disappointment of Kyle's career. Due to his surgery, he wasn't in tip-top condition as the Coyotes' training camp got underway. Dave Tippett had since replaced The Great One as coach, and rather than easing Kyle into the lineup, the Coyotes sent him to the San Antonio Rampage of the American League.

"I didn't skate until mid-August that summer and wasn't able to work out," Kyle said. "Physically, I felt I would be in good shape to start the season. Tippett came in as coach. He wanted to start from scratch, and I was sent to the minors."

Although he made a full recovery, Kyle spent the entire year in the AHL and played sparingly the following season with Phoenix, leading to his eventual move to the Senators.

"Coming to Ottawa was like a second chance," Kyle said. "I was so thankful to get it." **- MURRAY PAM**

MY FAVORITE...

TV shows: *Modern Family, Seinfeld, The League*

Actor: *Matt Damon. I love the Bourne series*

Actress: *Rachel McAdams*

Music: *Country. It puts you in a good mood. Also relaxing music such as Jack Johnson. I'm into a bit of everything*

Pre-game meal: *A mountain of pasta, preferably an alfredo and marinara mix in a rosé sauce topped with a chicken breast*

Video game: *I don't really play anymore, but I used to be into Madden Football and The Bigs*

Sports other than hockey: *Lacrosse. I'm a sports geek. I also like football and golf*

Players growing up: *Steve Yzerman, Mike Modano*

Team growing up: *Vancouver Canucks*

Way to score a goal: *There's nothing like scoring a goal in OT, especially in the playoffs*

WORD SEARCH

MURRAY
CHRIS NEIL
LEHNER
ANDERSON
SPEZZA
MELNYK
MACLEAN
FINNIGAN
BOBBY RYAN
SILVER SEVEN
ALFREDSSON
YASHIN
PHILLIPS
KARLSSON

C	H	R	I	S	N	E	I	L	K	E	D	M
Y	L	T	B	O	B	B	Y	R	Y	A	N	C
D	S	A	U	D	U	A	K	S	N	C	O	S
N	I	N	P	O	S	K	L	S	L	I	S	N
W	L	G	H	H	N	A	Z	Z	E	P	S	M
N	V	E	I	Y	A	R	R	U	M	H	D	A
I	E	N	L	B	N	L	H	L	M	O	E	E
S	R	C	L	J	D	S	S	E	A	R	R	D
O	S	X	I	H	E	S	P	H	C	A	F	L
J	E	U	P	O	R	O	U	N	L	C	L	E
H	V	V	S	N	S	N	Z	E	E	H	A	C
Y	E	P	O	U	O	D	L	R	A	E	N	U
K	N	A	G	I	N	N	I	F	N	K	M	H

→ *My First*
GAME

April 3, 2008
Phoenix Coyotes **4**
@ Dallas Stars **2**
5 shots, 19:28 ice time

KYLE
TURRIS

"My parents flew into Phoenix for the game. It was a surreal moment having coaches Wayne Gretzky, Ulf Samuelsson and Grant Fuhr behind me on the bench. Hopping over the boards and going up against Mike Modano was a neat experience. During a TV timeout, I would usually go to the bench to hang out, but I was struggling on faceoffs and went to the dot early. 'Mikey Mo' came in with me. We had a little chat. It was something I'll never forget, something I am thankful for. He welcomed me to the league."

CROSSWORD

ACROSS

1 Bryan ___ is general manager
3 Cody Ceci and No. 1 Down are local boys, both of them ___ natives
7 Eugene Melnyk is Ottawa's ___
8 Much-loved Roger ___ had a stint as an assistant coach
9 Abbreviation for the National Collegiate Athletic Association
11 Robin Lehner doesn't leave home without his ___
14 Where Jason Spezza played his junior hockey
16 ___ Anderson, pictured, is the Senators starting goalie
17 Ottawa's old NHL team was known as the ___ Seven
18 Goes in

DOWN

1 Marc ___ is on defense
2 Chris Phillips is one of several Senators who hail from this province
4 Daniel Alfredsson is Ottawa's career leader in ___, with 682
5 Not feeling well, and so less than 100 percent
6 ___-Gabriel Pageau is another local boy
10 An NHL Division, but it's not Ottawa's (the Senators are in the Atlantic)
11 Paul ___ is behind the bench
12 Takes a series 4-0
13 Clarke MacArthur and the departed Joe Corvo were signed as free ___
15 Bobby ___ was acquired in a trade with Anaheim

Mascot
"Spartacat"

AHL Affiliate
Binghamton Senators

FAST FACTS

Captain: *Vacant*

Coach: *Paul MacLean*

GM: *Bryan Murray*

Arena: *Canadian Tire Centre*

Capacity: *19,153*

Stanley Cups: *0*

Playoff Appearances: *14*

First Season: *1992-93*

CLAUDE GIROUX

IT'S NOT THE SIZE OF THE HOCKEY PLAYER IN the fight, it's the size of the fight in the hockey player.

Growing up in Hearst, Ont., Claude Giroux was small, but he displayed a big heart. Not only was he a bit on the small side, even for kids his own age, but he was always playing against boys older than him. He had to learn to keep his head up. At least once a game, some older kid would try to point out, with a shoulder or elbow, that he was playing with the "big guys" now.

Claude learned never to back down. Today, as captain of the Philadelphia Flyers, he continues to play that fearless brand of hockey he developed in his formative years.

"He was like Danny Briere...willing to go into the pack and then wait for things to open," said Claude's dad, Ray Giroux. "He was always playing with kids who were two or three years older than him, so he's used to playing with big boys. It was a positive thing. Now it doesn't bother him, because it's been like that since he was a kid."

Claude, who was considered one of hockey's three most valuable players in 2013-14, doesn't pause when asked to give his best trait.

"Courage," he said. "That was the hardest thing for

COURAGE WAS THE HARDEST THING FOR ME. I'M A SMALL GUY SO I NEEDED TO WORK HARDER THAN THE OTHERS

me growing up. You have to learn to be smarter. I'm competitive, a battler. I'm a small guy, so I need to work harder than the other guys."

At 172 pounds, Claude is lighter than nearly every one of his Flyers teammates. But he's learned how to navigate through the dangerous areas of NHL rinks by staying on his toes, just like his former mentor, the 5-foot-9 Briere, has been doing for many years.

Claude began skating and playing hockey when he was just two or three years old.

"Where I'm from, everybody plays hockey," he said. "That's what we're born to do."

It was more than just the love of getting up on Saturday morning, lacing up the skates and pushing a puck around the ice that attracted him to the game. He loved the angles, the motion and the way the game stimulated him mentally.

"Creativity," he said when asked how hockey caught his fancy. "You have to be smart to play the game. You can see the game any way you want."

Claude and his mates were on the ice every spare minute of every winter day. And when temperatures got down to, say, 40 degrees Celsius below zero, even the Hearst boys knew when to say when.

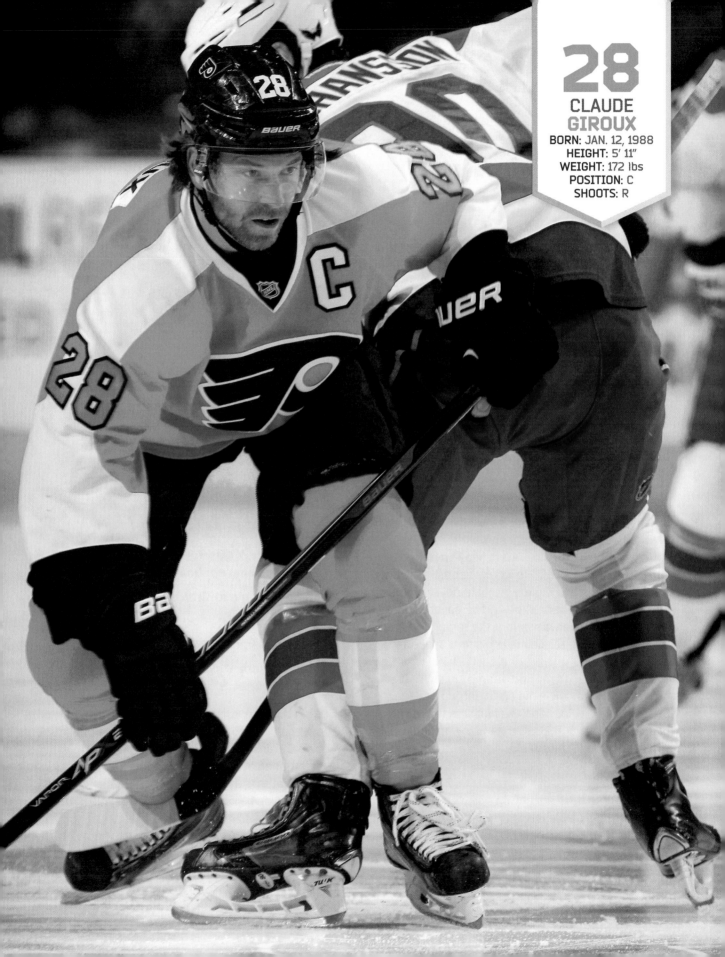

28

CLAUDE
GIROUX

BORN: JAN. 12, 1988
HEIGHT: 5′ 11″
WEIGHT: 172 lbs
POSITION: C
SHOOTS: R

"Yeah, me and my buddy had an outdoor rink and when it got too cold, we would play in his basement," said Claude with a laugh.

Despite his lack of size, Claude recalls actually splitting time between forward and defense in his early years.

"It didn't make any difference to me," he said.

By all accounts, Claude was a popular player growing up and had a knack for getting the best out of his teammates.

"He always wanted to win, but he played fair," his dad said. "The kids always wanted to play with him. It's all about making friends and earning respect from others."

By the time Claude reached the Quebec League as a member of the Gatineau Olympiques, the word was already out that this was a kid to watch. Small, said the scouts, but a fierce competitor.

"After a bad game, he wouldn't say anything verbally," Ray recalled. "He would just be in his own bubble. 'Don't disturb me.' He would never blame a loss on a teammate or a ref. And he never counted his points. It was always about the team."

Claude topped 100 points in his first season, 2005-06.

"Halfway through my first year in junior," Claude said, "there was talk in the air of getting drafted."

The Flyers did, indeed, take him with their first pick, 22nd overall in 2006. The wait was finally over.

"It was good," Claude said. "I was a little bit stressed, and that kind of relaxed me."

In his final season of junior, 2007-08, Claude led Gatineau to the President Cup and won the Guy Lafleur Trophy as playoff MVP. His dad said Claude makes a good leader, because he's always trying to learn and get better at what he does.

"He said that when he's done with hockey, he's

MY FAVORITE...

Movie: *The Wolf of Wall Street*

TV show: *Modern Family*

Band: *AC/DC*

Celebrity: *Will Ferrell*

Pre-game meal: *Grilled cheese sandwich*

Junk food: *Fries*

Player growing up: *Doug Gilmour*

Team growing up: *Montreal*

Sport other than hockey: *Basketball*

Hockey memory: *2010 Stanley Cup final*

Way to score: *Deke*

going to be coaching," Ray said. "It wouldn't surprise me if he does coach. As a boy, he would push others to go the limit."

All that said, Claude is still a fun-loving fellow who appreciates the child-like spirit of hockey. Asked what advice he would give to a young player today, Claude smiled.

"Just have fun out there during the game," he said. "Don't take it too seriously. Go out there and enjoy the game." – **WAYNE FISH**

WORD SEARCH

WELLS FARGO
ALLEN
RAY EMERY
ED SNIDER
BERUBE
PARENT
HOLMGREN
CLARKE
STEVE MASON
GIROUX
LEACH
FRED SHERO
MARK HOWE
TIMONEN

H	P	O	G	R	A	F	S	L	L	E	W	Z
T	J	P	E	L	P	E	C	N	E	L	L	A
W	Y	A	S	N	N	I	H	E	N	N	R	L
E	V	R	R	O	K	C	L	N	G	A	A	Y
F	R	E	D	S	H	E	R	O	I	L	Y	R
I	N	N	Z	A	B	D	T	M	R	F	E	S
D	E	T	B	M	Z	S	Z	I	O	E	M	J
E	R	K	E	E	B	N	E	T	U	K	E	O
T	G	N	R	V	R	I	L	T	X	R	R	K
R	M	O	U	E	V	D	S	E	T	A	Y	S
O	L	R	B	T	L	E	A	N	A	L	E	S
M	O	U	E	S	T	R	O	N	C	C	R	H
Y	H	M	A	R	K	H	O	W	E	N	H	I

My First GAME

February 19, 2008
*Philadelphia Flyer **2**
@ Ottawa Senators **3** (SO)
minus-1, 9:27 ice time*

CLAUDE
GIROUX

"I remember the warmup. It went really fast and that scared me. I had a lot of family and friends there because I grew up in Ontario and they made the trip down. I was really nervous. It took a while to settle things down. I just tried to think about what was happening on the ice. But it went well. I think I played OK, and when the game ended after overtime I shot first against Ray Emery. That was a lot of fun."

CROSSWORD

ACROSS

1 Craig ___ is now coach
3 Wayne Simmonds played for this junior team
7 Trailing teams will opt for an ___ attacker late in games
8 'The ___ on Ice' in 1980 is still fondly remembered, but it was the Flyers who really taught the Soviets a lesson in 1976
9 Joel ___ won a Cup with Calgary, then joined the Flyers
11 ___ Keenan coached a number of NHL teams, including the Flyers
14 He had four 50-goal seasons for the Flyers, still a team best
16 Philly drafted ___ Laughton 20th overall in 2010, pictured
17 Scrap or fight, like the Flyers of old often did
18 Claude Giroux hails from this Ontario town

DOWN

1 Bill ___ was both captain and coach in Philadelphia, and his No. 7 is retired by the club
2 Philly beat this team for its second Stanley Cup
4 Jakub ___, pictured
5 Giroux was the team's top ___ in 2012-13
6 ___ Hall is on the wing
10 Kimmo ___
11 Shoot wide or fan altogether
12 Mark ___ is on defense in Philly
13 In their heyday, the Flyers were known as 'The Broad ___ Bullies'
15 Matt ___ is on the wing in Philly

AHL Affiliate
Lehigh Valley Phantoms

ECHL Affiliate
Reading Royals

FAST FACTS

Captain: ***Claude Giroux***

Coach: ***Craig Berube***

GM: ***Ron Hextall***

Arena: ***Wells Fargo Center***

Capacity: ***19,573***

Stanley Cups: ***2***

Playoff Appearances: ***37***

First Season: ***1967-68***

SIDNEY CROSBY

CLOSE YOUR EYES AND THINK ABOUT BITING into a chocolate chip cookie. You taste the sweet cookie dough, and the chocolate chips start melting in your mouth. They're so good that you might not even bother to wipe the crumbs from your chin.

Now think about something you love to do, something you want to be really good at, even if it means you have to give up eating chocolate chip cookies. That's Sidney Crosby's world.

A big reason for his success with the Pittsburgh Penguins in the NHL and for Team Canada at the Winter Olympics is that he learned at a young age that he had to be dedicated. For years, he's been giving up things like chocolate chip cookies in favor of healthy food.

"I love chocolate chip cookies," Sidney said. "There's nothing better than my mom's homemade chocolate chip cookies. It's the brown sugar. She used to put extra brown sugar in there. Just thinking I had to give those up wasn't a good feeling, but that's what you've got to do sometimes."

By the time he'd turned 27 years old, Sidney, captain of the Penguins, had won a Stanley Cup, two Olympic gold medals, two NHL scoring titles and two Hart Trophies. From the time he was barely old enough to be in school, it was clear he was a good athlete and a great hockey player. He had his first interview with a reporter when he was seven.

Growing up, Sidney spent hours in his basement in Cole Harbour, N.S., shooting pucks at an empty net. Sometimes he missed it, which is why the nearby dryer was full of dents.

Sidney's mother, Trina, said that when Sidney got to be about 13 or 14 – "around the same time as when the social life kicks in" – he often skipped parties and other activities with his friends to meet his responsibilities, practise hockey or to go to bed early if he had a game the next day.

"He understood all of the things he was accountable for," Trina said.

Sidney has always loved hockey, so he really didn't mind. He thinks it'd be the same for kids who might be interested in being firefighters or writers or anything else.

"To achieve anything, you have to feel like you've sacrificed something," Sidney said. "I don't think anything you want in life necessarily comes easily. It doesn't have to be playing in the NHL. I mowed lawns or did landscaping stuff when I was younger so I could make money to play hockey. I had to sacrifice maybe going to play with my friends so I could have a job, like doing a flyer delivery route I hated."

> TO ACHIEVE ANYTHING, YOU HAVE TO FEEL LIKE YOU'VE SACRIFICED SOMETHING

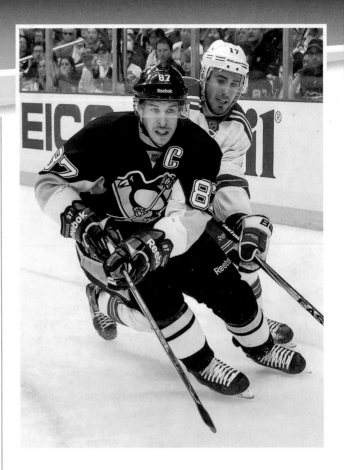

Sidney's father, Troy, insisted that his son do well in school. In 2002, when Sidney was just 15, he moved a long way from home to go to school in Minnesota at Shattuck-St. Mary's, North America's top prep school for future pro hockey players.

A year later, he started his first of two seasons of junior hockey in Rimouski, Que., with the Oceanic of the Quebec League. While he lived there, he finished high school and learned to speak French fluently. Even after Sidney was drafted first overall by the Penguins in the summer of 2005, shortly before his 18th birthday, he didn't want to simply assume he'd play in the NHL and be successful.

"It wasn't until the day I played," he said. "As much as I wanted to, and as hard as you work to do it, there are no guarantees. Whatever it is, you work as hard as you can, you have fun doing it and if you make it, great."

It hasn't always been easy. He's missed long stretches of games because of injuries, which has been frustrating, but he comes back strong. If you've seen Sidney during games, you know he can be intense.

"He's just very competitive," Trina said. "He's driven. He's more shark-like – he's relentless on the ice."

When he's not playing hockey, Sidney likes to hang out with friends, maybe plop on the couch and watch football, just like anyone else. He has a good sense of humor and is good-natured, upbeat and polite. He patiently signs autographs and poses for pictures with fans nearly every day. He's especially generous with his time when he meets people who face challenges, such as wounded military veterans or children who are ill.

"That's just the way God made him," Trina said. "Even as a baby, he would wake up with a smile on his face." **- SHELLY ANDERSON**

MY FAVORITE...

Band: *Great Big Sea*

Celebrity: *Russell Crowe*

Video game: *GoldenEye*

Pre-game meal: *Spaghetti with meat sauce*

Junk food: *Cheesecake*

Player growing up: *Steve Yzerman*

Team growing up: *Montreal*

Sport other than hockey: *My second-favorite to play would be baseball. My second-favorite to watch would be football*

Hockey memory: *My two years of junior in Rimouski*

Way to score: *Top shelf, glove side. It doesn't happen that often. That's why it's my favorite*

WORD SEARCH

H	F	Z	U	M	U	S	O	F	F	E	C	B
G	O	L	Y	M	P	I	C	S	F	R	S	E
I	C	B	E	S	X	E	V	I	O	K	N	P
L	R	F	V	U	A	T	C	S	H	U	E	L
S	J	L	I	T	R	A	B	X	R	N	V	C
O	O	Z	P	T	K	Y	X	U	H	I	E	V
H	H	S	A	E	F	S	T	E	E	T	T	O
N	N	B	T	R	S	J	L	I	A	Z	S	D
M	S	T	R	A	U	E	I	M	S	P	Y	B
Z	T	Z	I	I	H	B	L	E	T	A	N	G
Y	O	T	C	E	R	O	O	L	G	I	Y	T
R	N	I	K	L	A	M	A	M	E	R	O	Y
I	R	U	T	H	E	R	F	O	R	D	S	K

CROSBY
LETANG
IGLOO
FLEURY
RUTHERFORD
LEMIEUX
KUNITZ
SUTTER
JOHNSTON
MALKIN
EHRHOFF
OLYMPICS
STEVENS
PATRICK

My First GAME

October 5, 2005
Pittsburgh Penguins **1**
@ New Jersey Devils **5**
1 A, 15:50 ice time

SIDNEY CROSBY

"I remember just how anxious I was – how nervous but also how excited. You don't realize then that there are going to be 81 other games. It feels like that one is the most important, the biggest you'll play. It's a lot of fun. You think about a lot of things – about how hard you worked but also the people who got you to that point. I remember it was Mario Lemieux's birthday. I played with Mario, Mark Recchi, John LeClair. My first shift, I had a chance against Martin Brodeur. All those things combined were a big eye-opener."

CROSSWORD

ACROSS

1. 'Sid the Kid'
3. Dan ___ won a Stanley Cup with Pittsburgh in 2009
7. Former goalie ___ Johnston coached and managed the Penguins
8. Kevin ___ is the most penalized Penguin ever
9. When there's a ___ on goal, Marc-Andre Fleury is usually there to stop it
11. Crosby is on a ___ with Chris Kunitz
14. No. 17 Across played with the ___ team in Sochi
16. No. 11 Down was known as '___ the Magnificent'
17. ___ Malkin, pictured
18. Do what the NHL did in 1967, when Pittsburgh joined

DOWN

1. Paul ___ got 113 points one season, a record for a Pittsburgh defenseman
2. Beau ___ is a California boy
4. Brandon Sutter's number
5. Help in the scoring of a goal, like Crosby often does
6. Jaromir Jagr is one of four Pens to win the Art ___ Trophy
10. Jeering
11. The first Penguin to lead NHL scorers
12. Michel ___ was the first Penguin to have his number retired (he wore 21)
13. Used one's stick to impede an opponent
15. Pascal Dupuis' number

Mascot
"Iceburgh"

AHL Affiliate
W-B/Scranton Penguins

ECHL Affiliate
Wheeling Nailers

FAST FACTS

Captain: **Sidney Crosby**

Coach: **Mike Johnston**

GM: **Jim Rutherford**

Arena: **CONSOL Energy Center**

Capacity: **18,387**

Stanley Cups: **3**

Playoff Appearances: **29**

First Season: **1967-68**

T.J. OSHIE

LONG BEFORE T.J. OSHIE WAS STANDING AT center ice at the 2014 Winter Olympics with a game against Russia riding on his shootout performance, he was a penny-pinching college hockey player who had a restaurant appetizer on the line. Before Oshie ever donned the sweater of the St. Louis Blues or Team USA, he played at the University of North Dakota, which held a weekly shootout challenge. If you converted your attempt, you continued to the next round, and the last player standing was the winner.

"Thursday nights, we'd have the team meal on the road, usually at an Outback Steakhouse," T.J. said. "So we'd do the shootout every Thursday, and everyone on the team shot. If you won, you'd get a free appetizer that night. That was like $10, and in college, that's huge."

What dish did T.J. typically choose?

"The Bloomin' Onion."

It was an appropriately named treat for a late bloomer who was only locally recognized in St. Louis before bursting onto the scene in Sochi, where he converted four of six shootout attempts to help the United States edge Russia, 3-2.

"Sochi put him on the map, but he's been doing that for a long time, with North Dakota and St. Louis," said Chris Porter, who was T.J.'s teammate at

UND. "He's obviously a special player."

T.J. perhaps never envisioned singlehandedly beating the Russians at the Olympics, but he claims he always had confidence that he'd play hockey for a living.

"In the back of my mind, I always said that I was going to play in the NHL," he said. "I never knew what it took. I didn't really know if it was going to come true, but it always just seemed like it was going to happen."

The journey for T.J. included its share of pitfalls, and in the end it took a player who had more well-rounded ability than simply being a shootout specialist. His success perhaps stemmed from always playing against older and bigger competition.

> IN THE BACK OF MY MIND, I ALWAYS SAID THAT I WAS GOING TO PLAY IN THE NHL

"I was playing against guys who had facial hair when they were 15 years old and I was 14," T.J. said. "They already went through puberty, and I was this little kid who didn't go through puberty until college. You just learn that you have to work harder than everyone else just to keep up."

T.J.'s career sprang forward as a sophomore at Warroad (Minn.) High School, after his cousin, Cory Baudry, was killed in an automobile accident. T.J. returned from the funeral and led Warroad to the Minnesota Class A state title in 2003, putting his

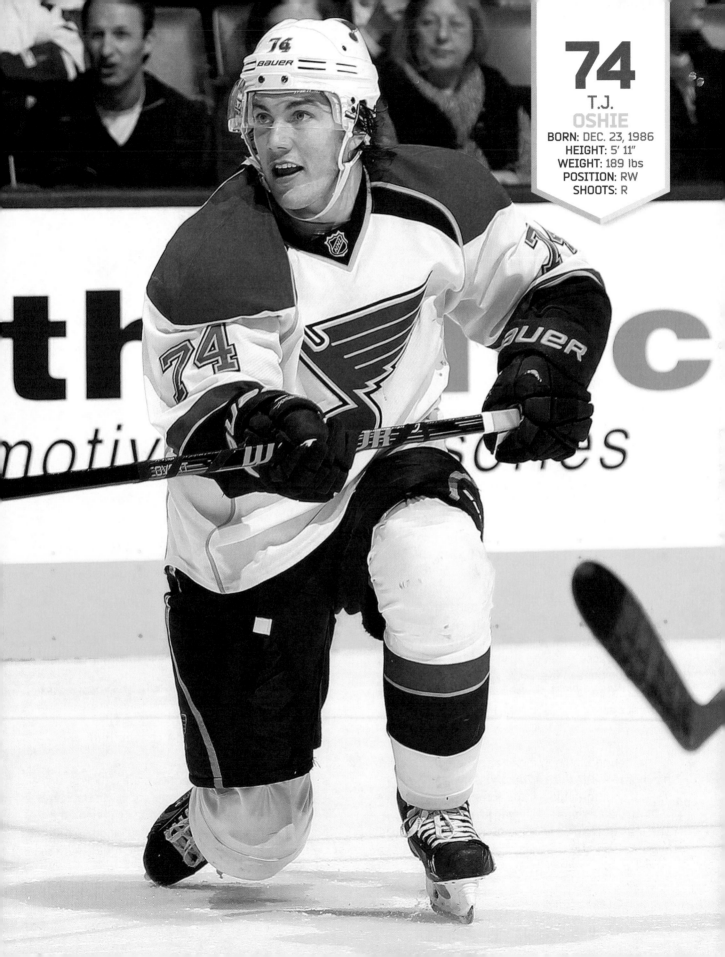

74

T.J.
OSHIE

BORN: DEC. 23, 1986
HEIGHT: 5' 11"
WEIGHT: 189 lbs
POSITION: RW
SHOOTS: R

name on the all-tournament team.

As a senior in 2005, T.J. totalled 99 points and helped Warroad to another state championship. His pro career took on some promise, too, when the Blues drafted him No. 24 overall that summer. He started his career at UND and began piling up more individual accolades, along with three consecutive appearances at the NCAA Frozen Four with the Fighting Sioux. After a 6-1 loss to Boston College in 2008, however, T.J. still wasn't sold on his future.

"We were playing BC in the Frozen Four and they beat us the two years prior," T.J. said. "I thought this was going to be the year. St. Louis is already saying they want me to sign. In the game, me and everyone else, we just played terrible. After that game, I was like, 'I don't think I'm ready to go pro. If I can't step up in a game here, how am I going to step up there?' It was really deflating."

T.J. did join the Blues the following season and began making a favorable impression on the ice, but not necessarily away from the game. In 2011, after a late night out, he overslept and missed practice, earning a two-game suspension from the club.

"That was rock bottom," T.J. said. "To the point where I was like, 'OK, do you want to party and have fun and be done in five years, or do you want to make a career out of this and hopefully never have to work again?' That summer, I got in really good shape and I've been building on that foundation ever since then."

That foundation now includes a memorable Olympic moment. His father, Timothy Oshie, was watching the shootout against the Russians back home.

"It made me remember when he was a little guy, and they would do a shootout at the end of practice," Timothy said. "He always took a lot of pride in shootouts. He was so small, and everybody thought he was

MY FAVORITE...

TV show: *Seinfeld*

Celebrity: *Denzel Washington*

Musician: *Luke Bryan*

Player growing up: *Wayne Gretzky*

Team growing up: *Dallas Stars*

Pre-game meal: *Chicken, pasta, white and red sauce and two sweet potatoes*

Junk food: *Peanut butter sugar cookies and Rice Krispies treats*

Video game: *Call of Duty*

Sport other than hockey: *Golf*

Hockey memory: *Winning the Minnesota state championship my senior year*

Way to score: *Breakaway or shootout*

so cute until he put four or five behind their goalie."

Team USA and Blues teammate David Backes added, "You're going to see T.J. Oshie become a household name after that display he put on."

Perhaps T.J. has paid for his last appetizer after all. – **JEREMY RUTHERFORD**

WORD SEARCH

E	M	A	U	N	A	M	W	O	B	S	O	K
H	I	T	C	H	C	O	C	K	R	E	U	S
N	V	T	E	J	L	E	S	R	J	K	E	S
G	E	O	T	G	N	S	U	E	C	C	P	C
N	M	I	S	M	N	E	T	D	R	A	L	H
O	O	L	L	U	H	T	T	E	R	B	T	W
R	W	L	E	K	E	L	E	F	E	Y	Y	A
T	A	E	A	B	G	I	R	R	E	N	O	R
S	I	N	N	I	C	A	M	I	T	N	C	T
M	L	A	Q	N	M	H	H	S	G	T	B	Z
R	I	B	I	N	R	S	A	N	H	I	L	Y
A	N	R	S	C	O	T	T	R	A	D	E	Q
I	L	I	N	S	S	R	N	F	O	W	D	K

BACKES

SUTTER

ARMSTRONG

ELLIOTT

STEEN

MACINNIS

OSHIE

BRETT HULL

HITCHCOCK

SCOTTRADE

FEDERKO

STASTNY

BOWMAN

SCHWARTZ

→ *My First*
GAME

October 10, 2008
*St. Louis Blues **5***
*@ Nashville Predators **2***
15:34 ice time

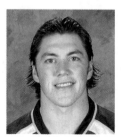

T.J.
OSHIE

"The game flew by, and I don't even know if we won our lost. I don't think I played very well. I was actually pretty bad. I don't think I did anything offensive or anything defensive very special. I just got through the game.

"I do have one memento from the game. St. Louis made me a little plaque with the game sheet, so that's floating around in the old garage somewhere. I don't really like keeping my awards out, so I just give them to my parents and they do whatever with them."

CROSSWORD

ACROSS

1. David ___ is the captain
3. Coach Ken Hitchcock won a Stanley Cup while behind the bench in ___
7. Sound
8. He's a shootout specialist
9. A pesky player or a difficult child
11. Aching
14. Barret ___ is an alternate captain
16. Big fight
17. Method of playing
18. The Blues picked up Ryan Miller and Steve Ott from this team at the 2014 trade deadline

DOWN

1. Scotty ___ was coach when the Blues went to their first Stanley Cup final
2. Brian ___, pictured, is between the pipes in St. Louis
4. An easy win
5. Brian ___ played for and later coached the Blues
6. Trophy won by former captain Chris Pronger in 2000
10. Bernie Federko holds many individual ___ in St. Louis, including most points and games played
11. Vladimir ___ is from the Czech Republic
12. Tosses out
13. Hitchcock also spent several seasons with this team
15. Maxim Lapierre scored this many goals in 2013-14

Mascot
"Louie the Bear"

AHL Affiliate
Chicago Wolves

ECHL Affiliate
Kalamazoo Wings

FAST FACTS

Captain: **David Backes**

Coach: **Ken Hitchcock**

GM: **Doug Armstrong**

Arena: **Scottrade Center**

Capacity: **19,150**

Stanley Cups: **0**

Playoff Appearances: **38**

First Season: **1967-68**

JOE PAVELSKI

JOE PAVELSKI DOESN'T GET DISCOURAGED EASILY.

"There was one time in grade school – I don't know what grade it was, maybe fourth or fifth – and the high school coach came in," he said. "When I told him I wanted to be a hockey player, he gave me that percentage – it might be one percent – who make it. But you're just a kid, you don't even know what that means."

And so he didn't give up on his dream. It came true, of course. Joe has reached hockey's highest level as a 41-goal scorer with the San Jose Sharks who's played in the 2010 and 2014 Winter Olympics with Team USA. But along the way, even those who helped him get there wondered if he had the skill set needed.

Joe grew up in Plover, Wis., a small town of 12,000. He was playing organized hockey by age six and later skated with the big guys on the backyard rink his older brother Jerry built every winter.

"I come from a great hometown, and everybody wants you to do well," said Joe, one of four kids in his family.

Hockey was important in the community, with the Panthers of Stevens Point Area Senior High the main attraction.

"However old you were, you wanted to go to the high school game because it was a big deal."

Joe was a freshman at Stevens Point and a big enough deal that he got a tryout with Team Wisconsin – a developing program that put the state's best players on one roster to compete against the best players in the country – a year earlier than the players he was competing against.

"Not the greatest skater and not the biggest," said Team Wisconsin founder Matt Carey, "but he had great hands and his hockey sense was off the charts."

Joe earned a spot on Team Wisconsin, but there still wasn't the expectation that he'd be a star or future NHL standout.

"He was not our top-rated player, because of his foot speed," Carey said. "Joe was middle of the pack. He was good enough to make the team, but he wasn't a top guy."

What Carey remembers most about Joe from those days was that he was a winner. In 2002, Joe led his high school team to a state championship. A week later, he was helping Team Wisconsin win state, regional and national titles – all in the same month. And it was during the semifinal game of that national tournament against Shattuck-St. Mary's, a powerful Minnesota prep team that featured future NHL players Zach Parise and Drew Stafford, that

> **JOE WAS MIDDLE OF THE PACK. HE WAS GOOD ENOUGH TO MAKE THE TEAM, BUT HE WASN'T A TOP GUY**

8

JOE PAVELSKI

BORN: JULY 11, 1984
HEIGHT: 5' 11"
WEIGHT: 190 lbs
POSITION: C
SHOOTS: R

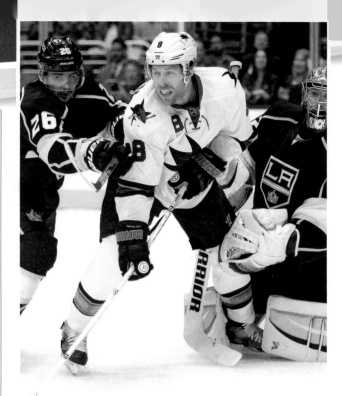

Carey and others realized how good Joe could be.

"When you saw him on the ice with all those other players, he could hold his own and then some," Carey said. "He could control the play."

Looking back, Joe – whose San Jose teammates call him 'Pokey' – said he was aware of concerns about his size and speed.

"You had an idea there were certain parts you had to work on – there was always the kid that could skate a million miles an hour and the kid that can shoot hard," Joe said. "You'd try to get better. The skating partly came with more strength. As you got stronger, you'd be a little bit better of a skater."

Junior hockey scouts followed Team Wisconsin, and Joe was soon moving up the ranks. He left Stevens Point before his senior year to play two seasons with the Waterloo Black Hawks of the United States League, then went on to play at the University of Wisconsin, where in 2006 he helped the Badgers to their first Frozen Four championship in 16 years. Joe was eligible for the NHL draft in 2003 after his first season in the USHL, but he wasn't a blue-chip prospect and didn't sit anxiously by the phone all day. Still, the Sharks grabbed him in the seventh round.

Joe was chosen as the Sharks' MVP for 2013-14 after leading San Jose with 79 points and those 41 goals. He's proven himself a versatile player, skating as a winger on the top line or as San Jose's third-line center. And that success reflects another trait seen in Joe as a boy.

"Every player has to understand his own strengths and weaknesses," Carey said. "Joe understands himself as well as any player out there. Most players in the NHL don't have the hockey sense he has. He works with what he has and that's important in life, not just hockey." **– DAVID POLLAK**

MY FAVORITE...

Movie: *Armageddon*

TV show: *Breaking Bad*

Musicians: *Kenny Chesney, Jason Aldean*

Celebrity: *Tiger Woods, in his prime*

Video game: *Growing up, it was R.B.I. Baseball on Nintendo*

Pre-game meal: *Chicken and pasta, mostaccioli*

Junk food: *Potato chips and Coke*

Player growing up: *Brett Hull. My brother liked him, but I liked the way he could shoot the puck and score goals*

Team growing up: *St. Louis Blues*

Sport other than hockey: *Golf*

Hockey memory: *Winning the championships: high school, USHL and college*

Way to score: *One-timer*

WORD SEARCH

MARLEAU
TORRES
COUTURE
ODGERS
DOUG WILSON
SAP CENTER
ANTTI NIEMI
THORNTON
PAVELSKI
BURNS
MCLELLAN
CHEECHOO
SHARKIE
OWEN NOLAN

I	K	S	L	E	V	A	P	M	V	E	C	B
G	O	W	E	N	N	O	L	A	N	R	S	E
I	C	D	E	O	D	G	E	R	S	E	N	M
M	R	O	V	U	A	T	C	L	A	R	E	C
E	J	U	I	K	T	H	B	E	L	U	V	L
I	O	G	P	O	K	O	X	A	J	T	E	E
N	Y	W	A	O	F	R	R	U	E	U	B	L
I	N	I	T	H	S	N	L	R	P	O	U	L
T	S	L	R	C	U	T	A	M	E	C	R	A
T	U	S	I	E	H	O	L	R	M	S	N	N
N	O	O	R	E	T	N	E	C	P	A	S	E
A	N	N	K	H	A	M	A	M	E	R	O	Y
I	H	C	I	C	S	H	A	R	K	I	E	K

→ *My First*
GAME
November 22, 2006
*Los Angeles Kings **3***
*@ San Jose Sharks **6***
1 G, 16:26 ice time

JOE
PAVELSKI

"I played with 'Patty' (Marleau) and (Steve) Bernier. 'Hanner' (Scott Hannan) took a shot – Mathieu Garon was in goal for the Kings – and it was a rebound and I put it in. I remember just getting to the rink and having that tired, dull feeling. You're excited, but it probably helps how tired you are, in a way, to calm you down. I didn't sleep much. I was getting tired, but I think I scored in the third period. It was awesome. I remember thinking, 'This is the NHL. These guys are big.'"

CROSSWORD

ACROSS

1 Number worn by No. 8 Across
3 A goalie who's pulled after a poor start gets an early ___
7 Guts or determination (sounds like an NHL trophy won by Joe Thornton in 2006)
8 He's an alternate captain in San Jose
9 What remains after a cut heals
11 Thornton also won the Art ___ Trophy in 2006
14 Sharks coach Todd McLellan also coached the ___ Aeros of the American League
16 Goalkeeper Antti ___, pictured
17 The Sharks won this many games in their second season
18 Thornton's hometown

DOWN

1 The Sharks won the Presidents' ___ for best overall record in 2009
2 San Jose is the ___ when NOT playing at the SAP Center
4 The Sharks' Tommy ___
5 Register (or make a phone call) (two words)
6 The Sharks dressing ___ is off limits to fans
10 Logan ___ is coming off another solid season
11 Collide with (two words)
12 When you ___ an opponent, you're looking at two minutes or more in the box
13 Doug ___ is GM
15 Martin Havlat wore this number when he played for the Sharks

Mascot
"SJ Sharkie"

AHL Affiliate
Worcester Sharks

FAST FACTS

Captain: *Joe Thornton*

Coach: *Todd McLellan*

GM: *Doug Wilson*

Arena: *SAP Center at San Jose*

Capacity: *17,562*

Stanley Cups: *0*

Playoff Appearances: *17*

First Season: *1991-92*

LIGHTNING

VICTOR HEDMAN

IT'S HARD TO BELIEVE VICTOR HEDMAN WAS ever the little guy, especially since he stands 6-foot-6 and weighs 223 pounds now. But growing up in tiny Ornskoldsvik, Sweden, Victor was the youngest of three boys and basement hockey games often ended with him running upstairs in tears.

"He liked to compete with his brothers," said Olle Hedman, Victor's father. "There was a lot of crying.... They were hard on him."

Victor, however, grew and grew, hitting the six-foot mark by the time he was 13 and continuing to shoot up. Despite being a small town, Ornskoldsvik is one of the most famous hockey spots in Sweden. Peter Forsberg, Markus Naslund and the Sedin twins all came from there, and it's where the Modo hockey team is based. Victor played for the Modo program all the way up through minor hockey and into the Swedish League. Along with Forsberg, some of his idols included Mattias Timander and Hans Jonsson.

"It's always special to put on the jersey of your hometown," Victor said. "Growing up, we were fortunate to look up to those guys."

His skills as a two-way defenseman made him a lock for the Swedish world junior team, and Victor won two silver medals in 2008 and '09 before starting his NHL career. That exposure, along with being named rookie of the year in the Swedish League, helped catapult him into the spotlight. With the second-overall pick in the 2009 draft, Tampa Bay nabbed a future cornerstone for its blueline.

A lot of expectations came with that pick, especially since the New York Islanders got John Tavares first overall and Colorado picked Matt Duchene third. Even on his own team in Tampa Bay, Victor would play alongside Steven Stamkos, who went first overall in 2008.

"My first year, 'Stammer' scored 50 goals," Victor said. "But I always felt like Tampa had faith in me."

Since those early days, Victor has matured and become the cornerstone the Lightning were hoping for. He's no longer the greenhorn on the blueline. "He's not afraid to take charge," said defenseman Mark Barberio. "There are times where he just breaks the puck out himself, and he doesn't need to make a pass because he's got such great wheels."

Even though the 2012-13 lockout was a bummer, it gave Victor a chance to grow in a different environment. He decided to get out of his comfort zone and went to play in the Kontinental League for Barys Astana, an organization based in Kazakhstan. He

> VICTOR'S CONFIDENCE IS THROUGH THE ROOF. IT'S ONE OF THOSE THINGS WHERE DEFENSEMEN TAKE A BIT LONGER

put up great numbers for the team and even earned defenseman of the month honors.

"It was a confidence boost," Victor said. "I got on the power play a lot, and even though it wasn't the NHL, there were things I could apply to my game when I got back."

Living in a different culture was a bit of a shock, since Victor had basically been limited to Ornskolds-vik and Florida until then.

"Astana was an eye-opener," he said. "Beautiful city, a lot of fans, and it was a good league. Some hotels and restaurants (around the KHL) were...not disgusting, but not far off. I had horse meat – that was disgusting. I will never eat that again."

Luckily for Tampa Bay, Victor started eating up opposing goalies and defenses once he returned from Kazakhstan. His shortened NHL season was solid, and in 2013-14 he posted career-highs with 13 goals and 55 points in 75 games. He'd never scored more than five goals in a season before that. The KHL experience helped, as did new coach Jon Cooper, who gave his defenders more freedom to roam up the ice and contribute in the offensive end. Victor got a lot out of that change in philosophy, and now he doesn't have to worry about being compared to the hotshot forwards drafted around him.

"His confidence is through the roof, you can totally tell," said goalie Ben Bishop. "It's just one of those things where defensemen take a bit longer."

If there was one big downer to his year, it was missing out on the 2014 Winter Olympics, where Sweden lost to Canada in the gold medal game. Victor was mysteriously left off the roster by Swedish management, but he used the snub as motivation once the NHL came back from the break. He also used the time to recharge his batteries by taking a vacation in the Caribbean. Even though he didn't

MY FAVORITE...

Movie: *Inglourious Basterds*

TV show: *The Blacklist*

Band: *Kings of Leon*

Celebrity: *Brad Pitt*

Video game: *FIFA 14*

Pre-game meal: *Rice, chicken and salad*

Junk food: *Pizza*

Player growing up: *Peter Forsberg*

Team growing up: *Colorado*

Hockey memory: *My first game*

Way to score: *Slapshot from the point*

get a chance to play in at the Sochi Games, Victor is always open to playing for the Tre Kronor.

"Absolutely," he said. "Playing for Team Sweden is always an honor."

The way Victor has developed, it's hard to imagine the Swedes passing on him again. **– RYAN KENNEDY**

WORD SEARCH

STAMKOS
BOLTS
ESPOSITO
FILPPULA
TIMES FORUM
COOPER
BEN BISHOP
THUNDERBUG
YZERMAN
ST. LOUIS
TORTORELLA
MATT CARLE
PALAT
LECAVALIER

B	R	E	I	L	A	V	A	C	E	L	S	H
Y	D	T	B	T	L	K	L	E	S	S	P	C
V	L	A	E	L	R	A	C	T	T	A	M	S
R	G	K	N	I	S	S	E	L	L	M	U	N
E	U	N	B	E	O	A	O	A	B	I	R	Y
J	B	A	I	S	K	B	T	N	E	F	O	K
O	R	M	S	N	M	N	L	S	R	I	F	W
G	E	R	H	S	A	H	P	I	E	L	S	N
A	D	E	O	N	T	O	I	T	P	P	E	I
F	N	Z	P	U	S	T	N	A	O	P	M	B
S	U	Y	V	I	J	S	T	L	O	U	I	S
E	H	I	T	U	E	D	N	E	C	L	T	D
N	T	O	R	T	O	R	E	L	L	A	M	H

→ *My First*
GAME

October 3, 2009
Tampa Bay Lightning **3**
@ Atlanta Thrashers **6**
1 A, 26:27 ice time

VICTOR
HEDMAN

"It was against Atlanta on the road. I still have the game sheet framed in my house. I took a shot from the blueline and 'Marty' (St-Louis) tipped it in. That was a good play."

CROSSWORD

ACROSS

1 Ben ___, pictured, is between the pipes
3 Jon ___ is behind the bench
7 Outfit
8 Take the place of another player, especially a goalie
9 First name of No. 1 Down
11 Sami ___ is a Finnish-born blueliner
14 ___ Lecavalier holds many team records
16 No. 1 Down was an Edmonton ___ earlier in his career
17 A fight is a ___-___
18 Victor ___ is a Lightning blueliner from Sweden

DOWN

1 He's an alternate captain in Tampa Bay
2 GM Steve Yzerman also ran the show for Canada at the ___ Games in Sochi
4 Former Bolt Teddy ___ is from Newfoundland
5 Tampa was ___-up in its division as recently as 2013-14 (that's to say, it finished second)
6 Number previously worn by Lecavalier
10 Former coach John Tortorella went on to coach this New York team
11 Birthplace of Tyler Johnson
12 Tied
13 College hockey's '___ Four' will take place at the Tampa Bay Times Forum in 2016
15 The Lightning had a whopping ___ in 2002-03

Mascot
"ThunderBug"

AHL Affiliate
Syracuse Crunch

ECHL Affiliate
Florida Everblades

FAST FACTS

Captain: **Steven Stamkos**

Coach: **Jon Cooper**

GM: **Steve Yzerman**

Arena: **Tampa Bay Times Forum**

Capacity: **19,204**

Stanley Cups: **1**

Playoff Appearances: **7**

First Season: **1992-93**

JONATHAN BERNIER

HOW DID JONATHAN BERNIER GROW UP TO play the game he loves so much? It's a story of brotherly love. If you trace the Toronto Maple Leafs goalie's career all the way back to his early childhood, many of his most important hockey moments involved a friendly sibling rivalry with brother Marc-Andre.

Marc-Andre, a right winger who currently plays professionally in France, is three years older, so he could tell his little brother what to do when they played road hockey growing up in Laval, Que.

"He always wanted a goalie to shoot at," Jonathan said. "That's how it started. I was a D-man when I was really young, and I switched when I was seven or eight years old. As soon as I put the pads on, I felt like that was my position to play."

Jonathan is a star in the NHL today with the Maple Leafs due to his quickness and athleticism but also because he handles the puck so well. And that skill also traces back to Marc-Andre. The Bernier boys wreaked havoc in their basement growing up as they practised their shooting together. Their target of choice was a freezer. They dented it with shot after shot.

"At first, my parents weren't too happy about it,"

> I NEVER TOOK IT REALLY HARD WHEN SOMEONE TOLD ME SOMETHING BAD. EVERYONE WAS PRETTY SUPPORTIVE

Jonathan said. "But they figured at least it was only that, and we didn't break any walls or too many things in the house."

Jonathan's parents, Alain and Lyne, were supportive as he grew up and not just because they put up with his and Marc-Andre's antics in the basement. They were their sons' biggest fans, taking them to practice and attending all their games. That's a big reason why Jonathan now honors all his family members in various tattoos. Every one represents each person's zodiac sign: a Virgin Mary for his mom (Virgo), Poseidon for his dad (Pisces) and water for Marc-Andre (Aquarius). Jonathan has a lion for his own sign, Leo, as well.

He rose up the junior ranks as a young goalie with the heart of a lion. His game took off in his second year of high school when he had a real goalie coach for the first time. On top of playing games, Jonathan received one-on-one instruction twice a week and improved rapidly.

He eventually broke into the Quebec League with the Lewiston Maineiacs in 2004. The starting goalie at the time was a now-familiar name: Jaroslav Halak. When some visa problems prevented Halak from travelling to Canada, Jonathan got the call to start. His opponent was the Halifax Mooseheads,

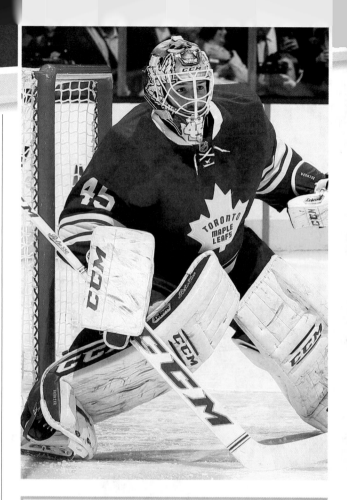

and guess who played for them at the time? It was Marc-Andre, who'd already been drafted by the Vancouver Canucks. Fitting, then, that Jonathan's brother became the first player to score on him in major junior.

"Sure enough, he scored on a rebound," Jonathan said. "So it's pretty funny. Exciting moment for my parents, obviously, to experience that."

Not one to let it go without some ribbing, Marc-Andre saved the fateful puck and gave it to Jonathan as a Christmas present. Perhaps the friendly taunting made Jonathan comfortable in his own skin. He was unflappable for the rest of his junior career, developing into one of the league's best goaltenders. He excelled in his first opportunity as a full-time starter the next season, and in 2006-07 he backstopped Lewiston to the QMJHL championship and a Memorial Cup berth. Team Canada took notice for the 2008 World Junior Championship, and Jonathan helped the team win gold.

The Los Angeles Kings were impressed with his puck-stopping ability and drafted him 11th overall in 2006. He won his first start with them the following year, played backup to Jonathan Quick en route to a Stanley Cup in 2012 and immediately excelled under pressure in the hockey-crazy city of Toronto after a 2013 trade brought him there. A big reason for his success was being comfortable with anyone who doubted him or gave him pointers on how to get better.

"You always actually grow as a player and a person if someone is tougher," he said. "I never took it really hard when someone told me something bad. Everyone was pretty supportive."

Talking to Jonathan, you get the sense everything rolls off his back. And he can thank his big brother for that. **– MATT LARKIN**

MY FAVORITE...

Movie: *Step Brothers*

TV show: *Suits*

Musician: *Avicii*

Celebrity: *Will Ferrell*

Video game: *EA Sports NHL series*

Pre-game meal: *Chicken parmigiana with pasta*

Junk food: *McDonald's*

Player growing up: *Patrick Roy*

Team growing up: *Montreal Canadiens*

Sport other than hockey: *Surfing*

Hockey memory: *2012 Stanley Cup*

Style of save: *Stacking the pads*

WORD SEARCH

DAVE KEON
LUPUL
SUNDIN
PHANEUF
TORONTO
HORTON
NONIS
CARLYLE
GARDENS
CARLTON
KADRI
WENDEL
SITTLER
GILMOUR

S	S	X	J	O	C	L	E	D	N	E	W	H
Y	L	W	R	T	L	T	Z	I	S	Z	O	W
H	F	U	E	N	A	H	P	S	M	R	M	S
R	A	N	Q	O	O	D	Z	V	T	I	V	N
C	R	O	L	R	E	A	R	O	L	L	D	E
A	L	N	B	O	A	V	C	N	M	A	D	D
R	S	I	T	T	L	E	R	A	Q	R	S	R
L	U	S	A	U	L	K	O	R	T	U	O	A
Y	E	X	P	R	X	E	R	L	E	O	K	G
L	T	U	J	U	D	O	E	T	W	M	E	U
E	L	V	Y	D	P	N	Z	O	S	L	I	S
Y	Q	X	T	Q	L	S	U	N	D	I	N	P
K	A	D	R	I	A	X	L	S	S	G	M	Q

→ My First
GAME

September 29, 2007
Anaheim Ducks **1**
@ Los Angeles Kings **4**
Win, 26 saves, .963 SP

JONATHAN
BERNIER

"It was in London, England, at the O2 Arena that just got built. It was such a big stage, and I almost can't even tell you what the final score was because I was so overwhelmed by it. I was so nervous. I got lucky and we got the win. You feel like you've achieved your dream. It was a blur, but at the same time I knew it was a big step for me. Playing a big game like that, gaining that confidence from my coach, starting the first game of the season and winning against the defending champs – that was something big."

CROSSWORD

ACROSS

1 The Maple Leafs play at the Air ___ Centre
3 James ___ was drafted by Toronto in 2006
7 Starts a game
8 Mats Sundin was a Leaf when Paul ___ was Toronto's coach
9 Syl ___ was a legendary Leafs captain
11 Something Jonathan Bernier wouldn't be without
14 Toronto traded for Dion ___, pictured, in 2010
16 Only Phil Kessel got more points than ___ Kadri in 2012-13
17 Where Sundin comes from
18 Area for goalies

DOWN

1 ___ Orr is a fan favorite
2 Suits up
4 Toronto's top farm team
5 Paul ___ played defense for Toronto in 2013-14
6 Every team needs a player who is "good in the ___"
10 Troy Bodie hails from Portage La ___
11 Dave Nonis is Toronto's general ___
12 Ignites
13 The Conn ___ Trophy is named after another Leaf legend, who was coach and owner
15 Number of Cups won by the Leafs in the 1960s (though they haven't won one since!)

Mascot
"Carlton the Bear"

AHL Affiliate
Toronto Marlies

ECHL Affiliate
Orlando Solar Bears

FAST FACTS

Captain: ***Dion Phaneuf***

Coach: ***Randy Carlyle***

GM: ***Dave Nonis***

Arena: ***Air Canada Centre***

Capacity: ***18,819***

Stanley Cups: ***13***

Playoff Appearances: ***65***

First Season: ***1917-18***

ALEXANDRE **BURROWS**

FOR YOUNG PLAYERS SHOOTING FOR THE stars, consider the tale of Alexandre Burrows.

The winding road to the NHL is full of slick stretches, potholes and enough debris to drive anybody into the ditch. And it's not so much that Alexandre endured the backroads of professional hockey from 2002 to 2004, on bus rides with the Greenville Grrrowl, Baton Rouge Kingfish and Columbia Inferno of the ECHL. It's how he clawed his way just to get into the American League with the Manitoba Moose.

It was 2004-05, and the NHL had begun what turned out to be a season-long lockout. Alexandre was 22 and playing for the Infero after stints with the Grrowl and Kingfish. He'd had three cracks at the Moose but was cut each time.

"I told myself if I was still on an ECHL roster by Christmas (2004-05) that I was going to pack it in and go back to university," he said. "It was a long road and it wasn't easy, but I'm glad it went that way."

In four games with the Inferno, Alexandre had five goals and six points, earning an early call-up to Manitoba, where he stayed the rest of the season. He debuted with the Vancouver Canucks in 2005-06, and then the following he signed his first one-way NHL contract.

Craig Heisinger, the Moose's general manager at

> I TOLD MYSELF THAT IF I WAS STILL ON AN ECHL ROSTER BY CHRISTMAS THAT I WAS GOING TO PACK IT IN

the time, is credited with finding Alexandre during a 2002-03 scouting trip. Had he not, Alexandre would've packed up his gear and perhaps transitioned into sports broadcasting, which still holds his interest as a post-hockey playing career path.

"It wasn't always easy for him," said Heisinger, now senior VP of hockey operations for the Winnipeg Jets. "If we said we thought Alex was going to be what he is today, we'd be lying. He's earned everything he's got. He's got to be having the time of his life."

During this time, as Alexandre was working his way up the NHL, he was living a bit of a double life. After two seasons with the Shawinigan Cataractes of the Quebec League from 2000 to 2002, he picked up ball hockey and won six national titles from 2002 to 2007. He's in the Canadian Ball Hockey Hall of Fame and the International Street and Ball Hockey Federation Hall of Fame.

"It helped me tremendously because it taught me at a young age to play against men," Alexandre said.

Now in his 10th NHL season, Alexandre has shown he can do just that, and then some. Some of his career highlights include scoring the Game 7 overtime winner in Vancouver's first-round series against the Chicago Blackhawks in 2011 and then the opening goal in a series-clinching win over the

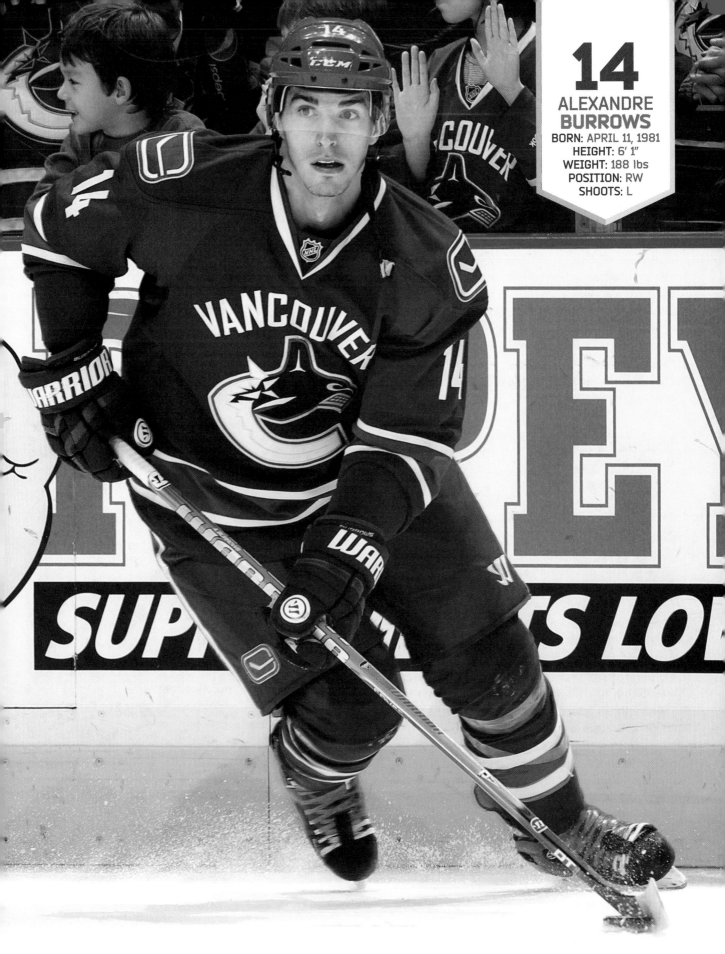

14

ALEXANDRE
BURROWS
BORN: APRIL 11, 1981
HEIGHT: 6′ 1″
WEIGHT: 188 lbs
POSITION: RW
SHOOTS: L

San Jose Sharks in the Western conference final that year. His flair for the dramatic started two years earlier, however, when he scored twice, including the overtime-winner, in the Canucks' first-round series-clinching win over the St. Louis Blues in 2009.

Still, there's always been a sense that Alexandre has had something to prove – that he was a replaceable winger on the top line with twin superstars Henrik and Daniel Sedin. Alain Vigneault, who coached the Canucks from 2006 to 2013, aligned

I'LL NEVER FORGET WHERE I CAME FROM. A LOT OF PEOPLE BELIEVED IN ME AND GAVE ME A SHOT

Alexandre with the Sedins in desperation Feb. 10, 2009. Trailing in the third period at St. Louis, Alexandre scored the tying goal en route to a 6-4 victory. The third-line checker and agitator became a first-liner that night, and on most after that.

Alexandre's best season came in 2009-10, when he had 35 goals and 67 points. By comparison, he had a season to forget in 2013-14, suffering a broken foot, jaw and thumb and totalling just 15 points in 49 games in the first year of an $18-million contract extension. In 2014-15, he'll have something to prove again, just like he did a decade ago.

"I'll never forget where I came from," Alexandre said. "A lot of people believed in me and gave me a shot." - **BEN KUZMA**

MY FAVORITE...

Movie: **_The Shawshank Redemption_**

TV show: **_Prison Break_**

Band: **_The Lumineers_**

Video game: **_Contra for Nintendo_**

Pre-game meal: **_Pasta, chicken, vegetables_**

Junk food: **_Burgers_**

Player growing up: **_Mats Naslund_**

Team growing up: **_Montreal Canadiens_**

Sports other than hockey: **_Tennis, football, baseball_**

Hockey memory: **_Scoring in Game 5 of the 2011 Western Conference final_**

Way to score: **_Forehand to backhand deke on breakaway_**

Alexandre
Burrows

14

VANCOUV

14

WORD SEARCH

SEDINS
MILLER
EDDIE LACK
HENRIK
LINDEN
TWINS
DANIEL
ODJICK
SANTORELLI
NASLUND
HAMHUIS
HARRY NEALE
STAN SMYL
ROGERS

O	Q	A	H	U	K	O	E	I	N	E	O	B
R	D	L	Y	Q	D	A	N	I	E	L	S	K
U	C	J	E	L	A	E	N	Y	R	R	A	H
T	R	F	I	D	A	R	C	L	B	A	N	L
H	S	L	L	C	E	E	O	I	D	A	T	C
H	E	N	R	I	K	L	F	N	E	I	O	L
R	D	A	U	H	F	L	R	D	W	M	R	Y
O	I	S	M	A	S	I	S	E	L	I	E	M
G	N	L	V	M	U	M	N	N	L	E	L	S
E	S	U	Q	H	O	H	C	Z	I	C	L	N
R	I	N	H	U	R	T	I	E	N	W	I	A
S	E	D	D	I	E	L	A	C	K	Q	T	T
I	E	P	U	S	Y	E	F	N	A	T	S	S

→My First
GAME

January 2, 2006
Vancouver Canucks **0**
@ St. Louis Blues **3**
2 shots, 7:23 ice time

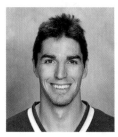

ALEXANDRE
BURROWS

"I got in during the afternoon, got on the bus and went to the game. I was star-struck. I didn't really play that many games at training camp, and then to see Trevor (Linden), 'Bert' (Todd Bertuzzi), 'Nazzy' (Markus Naslund) and 'Jovo' (Ed Jovanovski) – guys I really looked up to.

"I played with Jarkko Ruutu and Ryan Kesler, and I had a fight with Dennis Wideman at the end of the game. I kept my stick and brought it back to my parents' basement. It's still there. And I got the game sheet."

CROSSWORD

ACROSS

1 Daniel is one of the ___
3 The ___ Trophy is one of several never won by a Canucks player
7 How they say 'goodbye' in Alexandre Burrows' province
8 Number once worn by new president Trevor Linden
9 Schedule, as it's known in short
11 Both of the twins referred to in No. 1 Across have won the Art ___ Trophy
14 Pavel Bure was known as 'The ___ Rocket'
16 Ex-Canuck David ___ had his contract bought out in 2014
17 Daniel's brother, pictured
18 The Canucks play at ___ Arena

DOWN

1 Vancouver has a lot of Saturday and ___ home dates
2 Markus ___ also had his number retired by the Canucks
4 Fired bench boss John Tortorella previously coached this team
5 The Canucks have won their division many times and come ___ quite a few times, too
6 Experienced players
10 Zack ___ is on the wing
11 The Canucks sent goalie ___ Luongo to Florida
12 Stoop, like current Canuck goaltender Eddie Lack does
13 Covers closely
15 Number worn by No. 10 Down; it's been retired by many NHL teams

Mascot
"Fin the Whale"

AHL Affiliate
Utica Comets

ECHL Affiliate
Kalamazoo Wings

FAST FACTS

Captain: **Henrik Sedin**

Coach: **Willie Desjardins**

GM: **Jim Benning**

Arena: **Rogers Arena**

Capacity: **18,910**

Stanley Cups: **0**

Playoff Appearances: **26**

First Season: **1970-71**

NICKLAS BACKSTROM

A HOCKEY CAREER IS NEVER A STRAIGHT LINE.
Nicklas Backstrom has played professionally for
10 years now. He has been on teams in his native Sweden and in Russia, and has spent the past
seven seasons with the Washington Capitals. The
game has taken him to multiple Winter Olympics,
including a harsh disappointment in Sochi when an
allergy medication he was using caused him to fail
a drug test and receive a suspension for the gold
medal game against Canada. He's also competed in
more than 50 Stanley Cup
playoff games.

But Nicklas didn't simply
arrive in the NHL as a finished product. The Capitals
took Nicklas fourth overall
in the 2006 draft, but just
two years earlier he couldn't even crack the roster
on his own under-18 national team.

That's the memory that really drove Nicklas to
get better. He only started taking hockey seriously
at age 14, playing for Brynas (his hometown club in
Gavle, Sweden) and its junior team. He had a breakout season in 2004-05, with 17 goals and 17 assists
in 29 games, but that outburst came too late for
Nicklas, who was cut from the under-18 national
team camp the year before.

"You're not going to have your career go up and
up," he said. "There are going to be setbacks. I was

> YOU'RE NOT GOING TO HAVE
> YOUR CAREER GO UP AND UP.
> THERE ARE GOING TO BE
> SOME SETBACKS

17 when I first made it to the national team. Before
that I was just a regular player. I was lucky I didn't
make the national team. I got better and I didn't quit.
I just enjoyed playing and stuck with it. Hopefully, my
time would come, and it did."

Missing the cut for that 2004 team wasn't a surprise for a kid who was just 16 at the time. But Nicklas' goal had always been to play for the Tre Kronor,
and falling short was crushing. It was especially dis-
heartening because he knew he could compete with
the players who did make
it, a group whose average
age was 17.6 years old.

Of the 22 players who
made the under-18 team
for Sweden, which didn't
medal at the tournament,
only 10 were drafted by NHL teams, and only three
– forwards Tom Wandell and Niclas Bergfors and
defenseman Carl Gunnarsson – actually played in
the league. Bergfors was picked 23rd overall by the
New Jersey Devils in the 2005 draft. Wandell went
in the fifth round that summer to the Dallas Stars.
They were only nine and 11 months older than Nicklas when they made the team, but he had to wait
another year to prove he was as good.

"It doesn't end your career not making a team at
that age," Nicklas said. "I just worked harder, and
there were lots of people going in and out (of the

19

NICKLAS
BACKSTROM

BORN: NOV. 23, 1987
HEIGHT: 6' 1"
WEIGHT: 208 lbs
POSITION: C
SHOOTS: L

national team) at that time anyway. Players develop in hockey and as people. But I earned my way back."

During his breakout season with Brynas' junior team, Nicklas was recalled to the top club. Because he had a late birthday, he played 19 games in the Swedish League as a 16- and 17-year-old, some of them against elite competition thanks to an influx of players early in the season due to the NHL lockout.

In the spring of 2005, Nicklas helped Sweden to the bronze medal at the under-18 tournament, with two goals and three assists. By Christmas that same year he was with the under-20 team at the world juniors, where he had seven more points and set the stage for his selection by the Capitals. Sweden even played him in four games at the World Championship that May.

Nicklas credits his success to his parents, Anders and Christine, who never pushed him to play the sport. As a child, he could pick and choose which activity he wanted. It wasn't until he began serious training at 14 that he decided it was hockey and nothing else. It didn't hurt that Anders had played, too. He was drafted by the New York Rangers in 1980 and played professionally in Sweden with Brynas for nine years. When his son was worried about the direction his career was headed as a teenager, Anders was able to tell him how close he really was to realizing his dreams.

"We always had a good connection talking about hockey," Nicklas said. "We think about it in the same way. That's always a good thing. My dad had a big influence on my career. I had a lot of help from him. He was good that way because he wouldn't say anything to you. He would let me ask him and I always wanted to talk after the game. It was more me forcing him to talk." – **BRIAN MCNALLY**

MY FAVORITE...

Movie: *Gladiator*

TV show: *Suits*

Musician: *Avicii*

Video game: *Tiger Woods PGA Tour Golf*

Pre-game meal: *Spaghetti and meat sauce*

Junk food: *Hamburgers*

Swedish hockey team: *Brynas*

Player growing up: *Peter Forsberg*

Team growing up: *Capitals*

Sports other than hockey: *Soccer, NFL, golf*

Hockey memory: *Gold medal for Sweden at World Championship in 2013*

Way to score: *Slapshot*

179

WORD SEARCH

OVECHKIN
GARTNER
HUNTER
LANGWAY
SLAPSHOT
HOLTBY
MIKE GREEN
CHIMERA
LAICH
MCPHEE
BACKSTROM
MACLELLAN
TROTZ
VERIZON

Y	B	T	L	O	H	O	B	L	N	E	O	C
A	E	O	Y	Q	M	H	B	K	A	S	H	E
D	C	H	R	R	I	G	I	E	L	I	R	A
G	R	S	Q	D	K	L	M	P	M	O	C	L
M	C	P	H	E	E	J	O	E	D	V	N	H
T	X	A	L	O	G	A	R	T	N	E	R	Y
R	A	L	V	F	R	A	T	A	O	C	A	A
O	T	S	B	E	E	D	S	J	Z	H	M	W
T	S	T	R	E	V	K	E	I	K	O	G
Z	C	N	Q	A	N	H	C	Z	R	I	X	N
D	U	T	H	I	R	T	A	S	E	N	R	A
H	R	I	W	P	Y	T	B	U	V	T	T	L
I	E	P	N	A	L	L	E	L	C	A	M	D

→ *My First*
GAME

October 5, 2007
*Washington Capitals **3***
*@ Atlanta Thrashers **1***
1 A, 14:45 ice time

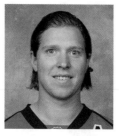

NICKLAS
BACKSTROM

"We played against Atlanta in 2007. It was a fun game. We won, so it makes it better. I was so nervous in the beginning, but after a while I relaxed and just tried to enjoy it. I'm pretty calm as a person so it worked out well. I didn't need any of the older players to do that for me. But it was a special moment. It was in Atlanta, though, so it's bad because we can't ever go back and play in that arena again in my career since the NHL moved the team to Winnipeg. That's how this business is, but it's weird."

CROSSWORD

ACROSS

1. He is in goal most nights for Washington, pictured
3. Where Alex Ovechkin was born
7. Overtime or ___ time
8. Gets by with what one has (two words)
9. The Capitals are the ___ team when NOT playing at the Verizon Center
11. Ovechkin switched to right ___ in 2013-14
14. Jason ___ is an Edmonton native
16. Joel Ward is from ___ York, Ont.
17. Where Nicklas Backstrom and Marcus Johansson hail from
18. ___ Laich is Washington's alternate captain

DOWN

1. Dale ___ is Washington's all-time leader in penalty minutes, with over 2,000
2. Karl Alzner is from ___, B.C.
4. John ___ is an American-born Capital
5. Tom ___ is a rugged winger
6. Former Capitals coach ___ Oates
10. A referee may 'put away his ___' in the late stages of a close game
11. Dustin Penner, a late-season pickup in 2013-14, is from ___, Manitoba
12. Washington employs a number of amateur ___ to look out for promising players
13. The Capitals upset this team in a shootout late in the season
15. Ovie's first name

Mascot
"Slapshot"

AHL Affiliate
Hershey Bears

ECHL Affiliate
South Carolina Stingrays

FAST FACTS

Captain: *Alex Ovechkin*

Coach: *Barry Trotz*

GM: *Brian MacLellan*

Arena: *Verizon Center*

Capacity: *18,506*

Stanley Cups: *0*

Playoff Appearances: *24*

First Season: *1974-75*

MARK SCHEIFELE

THE WAY MARK SCHEIFELE IS ABLE TO PROCESS opponents moving swiftly around him and still choose and execute the right plays, you'd assume the bright lights of the NHL had always called to him.

Not so much, actually.

It turns out that, not long ago, Scheifele was like a lot of high school kids. He couldn't make up his mind about what sport interested him most.

"Until I made it to the OHL, I played every sport," Mark said. "Badminton, basketball, volleyball, track and field, lacrosse. Hockey was just one of them."

Mark was an excellent athlete while a student at Grand River Collegiate Institute in Kitchener, Ont. He was a key performer on a championship junior boys basketball team, so no surprise that conflicts became inevitable. One situation may have given Mark the shove that propelled him to NHL prominence.

Around his 16th birthday, he was in the middle of the high school basketball season and playing with the Kitchener minor midgets on the ice. His hockey coach at the time, Todd Hoffman, remembers the important day.

"He was a very popular kid in school," he said. "They wanted him to play on all these school teams, basketball and what have you. I remember him coming to one of our practices one night, and he came to me and said he couldn't make tomorrow night's practice because of basketball."

Rather than getting angry, or even letting it slide, Hoffman decided to take a stand with Mark. He reminded him about what was said earlier in the year to the team and the parents about priorities, that the team and his teammates must come first. Hoffman pointed out to Mark it was the year he could be drafted to the OHL and that the minor midget hockey playoffs were also approaching.

"I said to him, 'Mark, I have no objection, if we weren't practising, for you to go play,'" Hoffman said. "'But you're a key player and if you want to be a hockey player, you need to make the decision on whether or not to play basketball or come to our practice.' At the end of the day, he came to practice. He made the commitment. His game took off from there."

Mark was a seventh-round pick by the Saginaw Spirit in the 2009 OHL draft but didn't make the team that fall. He played Jr. B in Kitchener under Hoffman, and when his OHL rights were traded to the Barrie Colts the next summer, he cracked the lineup and started his OHL career with a 75-point season.

> I WAS A TERRIBLE SKATER.
> I KIND OF RAN ON MY SKATES.
> I WASN'T THAT GREAT, BUT I
> TRIED MY HARDEST

The course was set, and that led to the Winnipeg Jets nabbing him No. 7 overall in the 2011 NHL draft. Mark can trace his becoming a self-proclaimed "hockey nerd" to about that time under Hoffman.

"I don't think I started loving the game like I do until I was 17," he said.

Especially since the start of his time in Barrie, Mark said that hockey occupies almost all of his day, both on the ice and in his head, with practices, meetings, games, video breakdown and analysis sessions and with games on TV even on off-days.

Yet for all his gifts and the focus he displays today with the Jets, success wasn't a sure thing, given his start in the game.

"When I was four, my parents couldn't even pull me onto the ice," he said. "I didn't want to go on the ice at all."

By the time he was seven, there were stressful tryouts for a local team. Only two cuts had to be made, and despite Mark's poor skating, he was kept on the team.

"I was a terrible skater," he said with a laugh. "I kind of ran on my skates, I wasn't that great. I tried my hardest, but I struggled with it early. I started to get a little more co-ordinated later, and I got to play with the same team through the rest of my minor hockey days, like for nine years, so that was fun."

Although many things have fallen into place, Mark knows he's still a work in progress. While he appeared to be a calm, patient rookie throughout 2013-14, concentrating on defense and waiting for his offense to emerge – even when he managed just one goal and five points in the first 24 games – he was really like a duck on water. It was smooth above while his feet were paddling furiously below.

"My parents are always on that," Mark said. "I can't handle waiting for something. If something gets on

MY FAVORITE...

Movie: *Miracle*

TV show: *Suits*

Musician: *Taylor Swift*

Celebrity: *Jennifer Aniston*

Video game: *Call of Duty*

Pre-game meal: *Chicken and rice*

Junk food: *Chocolate, any chocolate*

Player growing up: *Steve Yzerman*

Team growing up: *Detroit Red Wings*

Sport other than hockey: *Lacrosse*

Hockey memory: *My first NHL goal*

Way to score: *Breakaway*

my mind, I don't want to wait until two days from now to go do it. I want to do it that second. They're on me all the time about being so impatient."

– TIM CAMPBELL

WORD SEARCH

L	M	T	S	C	E	N	T	R	E	E	O	B
R	A	L	Y	Q	P	H	B	K	L	S	S	E
M	U	D	R	R	H	A	I	E	T	A	E	A
T	R	F	D	N	A	L	V	P	T	U	T	S
A	I	N	R	R	E	J	O	E	I	A	O	A
T	C	A	E	O	A	A	F	U	L	I	G	Y
N	E	I	L	G	U	F	Y	B	W	E	U	S
A	T	S	E	N	S	T	R	O	M	N	C	O
L	S	O	E	R	U	L	N	E	L	E	H	G
T	C	G	H	A	V	C	O	C	U	P	I	K
A	I	O	W	H	R	T	I	E	N	I	R	G
R	R	B	M	I	C	K	E	M	O	O	S	E
I	E	L	L	U	H	Y	B	B	O	B	S	K

BYFUGLIEN
MAURICE
MTS CENTRE
ENSTROM
LADD
PAVELEC
BOGOSIAN
ATLANTA
AVCO CUP
WHEELER
SETOGUCHI
MICK E. MOOSE
BOBBY HULL
LITTLE

→ My First
GAME

October 9, 2011
*Montreal Canadiens **5***
*@ Winnipeg Jets **1***
1 shot, 13:44 ice time

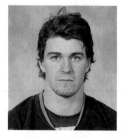

**MARK
SCHEIFELE**

"I could barely sleep the night before. I finally got to sleep and then came to the rink on that day. It seemed regular, but I was a little nervous. I had the butterflies, and I was really nervous when I got there. I did an interview – probably the worst interview I've ever done in my life. I didn't even know what I was saying. It was a terrible interview, and I was shaking the entire time. All I remember about the day was the nervousness. But I'd played my first NHL game. It ended up being a great memory."

CROSSWORD

ACROSS

1 Goalie ___ Pavelec, pictured
3 Bryan ___ plays big in Winnipeg
7 Shoot the puck really hard
8 Zach Bogosian plays ___
9 Jimmy ___ was a rugged Jet of the past and led the league in penalty minutes in 1979-80
11 Players with big ___ think too highly of themselves
14 Winnipeg has yet to host the NHL ___-___ Game
16 No. 11 Down is the only ___ with the Jets (they also have one Finn)
17 Hollered
18 The earlier edition of the Jets played in what was then known as the ___ Division

DOWN

1 Team that used to have the Jets' number at playoff time
2 Winnipeg used to belong to the NHL's ___ Conference
4 One of the NHL cities in which Paul Maurice coached before coming to Winnipeg
5 Matt Halischuk and No. 3 Across are among the shortest Jets at five-foot ___
6 Andrew ___ is Jets captain
10 Where the franchise was based before coming to Winnipeg
11 Tobias ___ is another blueliner
12 Former Jet Dale Hawerchuk won the ___ Trophy as the NHL's top rookie
13 The Jets play at the MTS ___
15 ___ Dudley was GM before Kevin Cheveldayoff took over

Mascot
"Mick E. Moose"

AHL Affiliate
St. John's
IceCaps

ECHL Affiliate
Ontario
Reign

FAST FACTS

Captain: *Andrew Ladd*

Coach: *Paul Maurice*

GM: *Kevin Cheveldayoff*

Arena: *MTS Centre*

Capacity: *15,004*

Stanley Cups: *0*

Playoff Appearances: *1*

First Season: *1999-00*

SOLUTIONS

Crosswords

Anaheim Ducks
ACROSS 1. MIGHTY, 3. ANGELS, 7. ALLEN, 8. FINESSE, 9. HALO, 11. SONS, 14. TALLIES, 16. LIBRA, 17. KARIYA, 18. REGINA.
DOWN 1. MURRAY, 2. TORONTO, 4. EMERSON, 5. SWEDEN, 6. LEAF, 10. ALL-STAR, 11. SELANNE, 12. STREAK, 13. CANADA, 15. SAKU.

Arizona Coyotes
ACROSS 1. VRBATA, 3. YANDLE, 7. SHANE, 8. LARSSON, 9. SALT, 11. RUSH, 14. ART ROSS, 16. BURKE, 17. GREISS, 18. MORRIS.
DOWN 1. VANISH, 2. TIPPETT, 4. DRESSES, 5. ENDING, 6. PAUL, 10. ANTOINE, 11. RIBEIRO, 12. LACING, 13. REBELS, 15. SUNS.

Boston Bruins
ACROSS 1. KREJCI, 3. TUUKKA, 7. EDGED, 8. WINGERS, 9. ROSS, 11. POST, 14. RAYMOND, 16. DRAFT, 17. SECOND, 18. IGINLA.
DOWN 1. KASPER, 2. CLAUDES, 4. KILLERS, 5. ASSIST, 6. DRAW, 10. OLYMPIC, 11. PADDING, 12. BRUINS, 13. OTTAWA, 15. DUMB.

Buffalo Sabres
ACROSS 1. ENROTH, 3. FRENCH, 7. NOLAN, 8. BUFFALO, 9. OHIO, 11. FRAY, 14. UNDRESS, 16. LEINO, 17. HENRIK, 18. BOSTON.
DOWN 1. ENDING, 2. TORONTO, 4. NIAGARA, 5. HORTON, 6. STAB, 10. HODGSON, 11. FOLIGNO, 12. PUNISH, 13. BOWMAN, 15. SHUT.

Calgary Flames
ACROSS 1. CREASE, 3. SUTTER, 7. APRIL, 8. TRAINER, 9. GARY, 11. ATOM, 14. ELBOWED, 16. LEAFS, 17. STAJAN, 18. JAROME.
DOWN 1. CORRAL, 2. STANLEY, 4. TORONTO, 5. ROBERT, 6. MATT, 10. ALBERTA, 11. ATLANTA, 12. DENNIS, 13. ASPIRE, 15. DAVE.

Carolina Hurricanes
ACROSS 1. TLUSTY, 3. PETERS, 7. VOTED, 8. PRIMEAU, 9. SCAR, 11. WINS, 14. MANAGER, 16. ALONE, 17. EXTEND, 18. OSHAWA.
DOWN 1. TWELVE, 2. THUNDER, 4. EASTERN, 5. SETS UP, 6. CAMP, 10. CONSORT, 11. WHALERS, 12. SMYTHE, 13. SEKERA, 15. RICK.

Chicago Blackhawks
ACROSS 1. MARIAN, 3. SAVARD, 7. TOEWS, 8. ATLANTA, 9. USES, 11. PETE, 14. WINDSOR, 16. THREE, 17. NEEDLE, 18. SKATER.
DOWN 1. MIKITA, 2. ASSISTS, 4. AGAINST, 5. DUNCAN, 6. AREA, 10. SAN JOSE, 11. PATRICK, 12. SWEDEN, 13. CENTER, 15. RUDY.

Colorado Avalanche
ACROSS 1. SEMYON, 3. BARRIE, 7. HOTEL, 8. GABRIEL, 9. CODY, 11. DISK, 14. EXECUTE 16. COACH, 17. TALBOT, 18. CENTER.
DOWN 1. SMYTHE, 2. O'REILLY, 4. ROCKIES, 5. EXCELS, 6. GREG, 10. OVERALL, 11. DUCHENE, 12. BENOIT, 13. SHINER, 15. ERIK.

Columbus Blue Jackets
ACROSS 1. MURRAY, 3. ARNIEL, 7. ALONE, 8. FOLIGNO, 9. WARM, 11. BELL, 14. EASTERN, 16. ARENA, 17. ANSWER, 18. UNEVEN.
DOWN 1. MARIAN, 2. ANAHEIM, 4. ILLEGAL, 5. LONDON, 6. LEAF, 10. ASSISTS, 11. BRANDON, 12. VEZINA, 13. CANTON, 15. NASH.

Dallas Stars
ACROSS 1. VALERI, 3. TRADES, 7. TEXAS, 8. HORCOFF, 9. AWOL, 11. JETS, 14. ACROBAT, 16. MAJOR, 17. SEGUIN,º 18. CLARKE.
DOWN 1. VISITS, 2. ROUSSEL, 4. DETROIT, 5. STRIFE, 6. RICH, 10. WARBURG, 11. JIM NILL, 12. SABRES, 13. FRANCE, 15. TIES.

Detroit Red Wings
ACROSS 1. NIKLAS, 3. ILITCH, 7. ISSUE, 8. REGULAR, 9. NORM, 11. HART, 14. ART ROSS, 16. SWEDE, 17. LESTER, 18. MRAZEK.
DOWN 1. NORRIS, 2. ANAHEIM, 4. TRAILER, 5. HOWARD, 6. FOUR, 10. OCTOPUS, 11. HUSTLER, 12. DANIEL, 13. HENRIK, 15. SENS.

Edmonton Oilers
ACROSS 1. JORDAN, 3. SMYTHE, 7. EAGER, 8. RUSSIAN, 9. NCAA, 11. HEEL, 14. ASSISTS, 16. PLACE, 17. REGINA, 18. USHERS.
DOWN 1. JERSEY, 2. ALBERTA, 4. TWO-TIME, 5. EAKINS, 6. FOUR, 10. CASHING, 11. HOPKINS, 12. GAGNER, 13. REBELS, 15. SALT.

Florida Panthers
ACROSS 1. JEROME, 3. BARKOV, 7. EAGLE, 8. BLOCKER, 9. STUN, 11. SAVE, 14. JOKINEN, 16. OUTDO, 17. SUTTER, 18. PETERS.
DOWN 1. JERSEY, 2. MacLEAN, 4. KULIKOV, 5. VISORS, 6. STAB, 10. TAKE OUT, 11. SCOTTIE, 12. EJECTS, 13. WOMEN'S, 15. NICK.

Los Angeles Kings
ACROSS 1. JARRET, 3. PARKER, 7. ICING, 8. SCRATCH, 9. USED, 11. TORE, 14. MANAGER, 16. ROGIE, 17. ELEVEN, 18. LONDON.
DOWN 1. JUSTIN, 2. ENGAGED, 4. KOPITAR, 5. REGEHR, 6. ROSS, 10. SAN JOSE, 11. TORONTO, 12. SMYTHE, 13. SEASON, 15. ROBS.

Minnesota Wild
ACROSS 1. PARISE, 3. NIKLAS, 7. TRAIL, 8. HARDING, 9. UGLY, 11. MEET, 14. CENTERS, 16. KOIVU, 17. SILVER, 18. FOUGHT.
DOWN 1. POINTS, 2. STANLEY, 4. LEMAIRE, 5. STINGY, 6. JOSH, 10. GENERAL, 11. MIKE YEO, 12. SCOUTS, 13. AUGUST, 15. STAR.

Montréal Canadiens
ACROSS 1. GIONTA, 3. SUBBAN, 7. GREEN, 8. SHORTEN, 9. TRIO, 11. MOEN, 14. LAFLEUR, 16. UPSET, 17. ELEVEN, 18. CENTRE.
DOWN 1. GEORGE, 2. TORONTO, 4. BRITTLE, 5. NAGANO, 6. CUPS, 10. REFEREE, 11. MAURICE, 12. PLANTE, 13. STRIDE, 15. RYAN.

Nashville Predators
ACROSS 1. FISHER, 3. VIKTOR, 7. CLUNE, 8. TIMONEN, 9. STUN, 11. NOOK, 14. BOURQUE 16. SMITH, 17. SCREEN, 18. SMYTHE.
DOWN 1. FRENCH, 2. EASTERN, 4. TORONTO, 5. RATING, 6. MATT, 10. THUNDER, 11. NYSTROM, 12. OBSESS, 13. CHANCE, 15. ERIC.

New Jersey Devils
ACROSS 1. DeBOER, 3. SCORES, 7. THREE, 8. LEMAIRE, 9. BARN, 11. JAGR, 14. GELINAS 16. RUUTU, 17. SERIES, 18. TRAVIS.
DOWN 1. DEBUTS, 2. EASTERN, 4. RAGGING, 5. SUTTER, 6. GOAL, 10. ALL-STAR, 11. JAROMIR, 12. AGENTS, 13. ZUBRUS, 15. SEED.

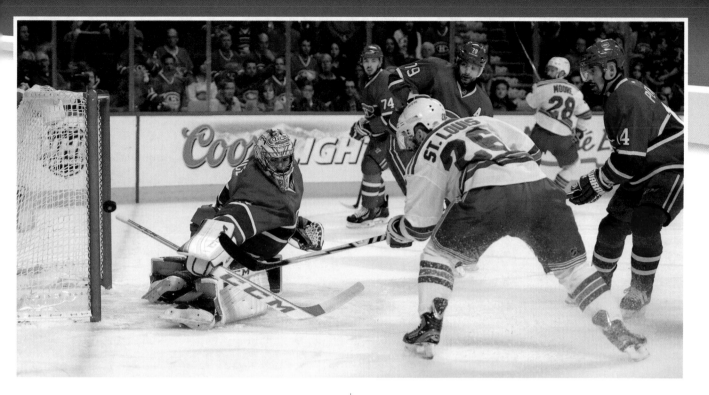

New York Islanders
ACROSS 1. EVGENI, 3. ST. PAUL, 7. TAKES, 8. STARTER, 9. JOHN, 11. CARP, 14. STYLISH, 16. PASTA, 17. ANCHOR, 18. TORREY.
DOWN 1. EIGHTY, 2. NIELSEN, 4. ALL-STAR, 5. LOSERS, 6. NETS, 10. OLYMPIC, 11. CAPUANO, 12. OSHAWA, 13. BAILEY, 15. HAAN.

New York Rangers
ACROSS 1. STEPAN, 3. SATHER, 7. ADAMS, 8. STANLEY, 9. UMPS, 11. GUNS, 14. ENDINGS, 16. RIGHT, 17. HENRIK, 18. MICHEL.
DOWN 1. STREAK, 2. ASSISTS, 4. HAGELIN, 5. RELAYS, 6. MATS, 10. MADISON, 11. GIRARDI, 12. LEETCH, 13. ST. PAUL, 15. STAR.

Ottawa Senators
ACROSS 1. MURRAY, 3. OTTAWA, 7. OWNER, 8. NEILSON, 9. NCAA, 11. MASK, 14. WINDSOR, 16. CRAIG, 17. SILVER, 18. ENTERS.
DOWN 1. METHOT, 2. ALBERTA, 4. ASSISTS, 5. AILING, 6. JEAN, 10. CENTRAL, 11. MacLEAN, 12. SWEEPS, 13. AGENTS, 15. RYAN.

Philadelphia Flyers
ACROSS 1. BERUBE, 3. BRAVES, 7. EXTRA, 8. MIRACLE, 9. OTTO, 11. MIKE, 14. TIM KERR, 16. SCOTT, 17. TANGLE, 18. HEARST.
DOWN 1. BARBER, 2. BUFFALO, 4. VORACEK, 5. SCORER, 6. ADAM, 10. TIMONEN, 11. MISFIRE, 12. STREIT, 13. STREET, 15. READ.

Pittsburgh Penguins
ACROSS 1. CROSBY, 3. BYLSMA, 7. EDDIE, 8. STEVENS, 9. SHOT, 11. LINE, 14. RUSSIAN, 16. MARIO, 17. EVGENI, 18. EXPAND.
DOWN 1. COFFEY, 2. BENNETT, 4. SIXTEEN, 5. ASSIST, 6. ROSS, 10. HISSING, 11. LEMIEUX, 12. BRIERE, 13. HOOKED, 15. NINE.

St. Louis Blues
ACROSS 1. BACKES, 3. DALLAS, 7. AUDIO, 8. T.J. OSHIE, 9. BRAT, 11. SORE, 14. JACKMAN, 16. BRAWL, 17. SYSTEM, 18. SABRES.
DOWN 1. BOWMAN, 2. ELLIOTT, 4. LAUGHER, 5. SUTTER, 6. HART, 10. RECORDS, 11. SOBOTKA, 12. EJECTS, 13. FLYERS, 15. NINE.

San Jose Sharks
ACROSS 1. TWELVE, 3. SHOWER, 7. HEART, 8. MARLEAU, 9. SCAR, 11. ROSS, 14. HOUSTON, 16. NIEMI, 17. ELEVEN, 18. LONDON.
DOWN 1. TROPHY, 2. VISITOR, 4. WINGELS, 5. RING UP, 6. ROOM, 10. COUTURE, 11. RUN INTO, 12. CHARGE, 13. WILSON, 15. NINE.

Tampa Bay Lightning
ACROSS 1. BISHOP, 3. COOPER, 7. EQUIP, 8. RELIEVE, 9. ERIC, 11. SALO, 14. VINCENT, 16. OILER, 17. DUST-UP, 18. HEDMAN.
DOWN 1. BREWER, 2. OLYMPIC, 4. PURCELL, 5. RUNNER, 6. FOUR, 10. RANGERS, 11. SPOKANE, 12. EVENED, 13. FROZEN, 15. TIES.

Toronto Maple Leafs
ACROSS 1. CANADA, 3. REIMER, 7. OPENS, 8. MAURICE, 9. APPS, 11. MASK, 14. PHANEUF, 16. NAZEM, 17. SWEDEN, 18. CREASE.
DOWN 1. COLTON, 2. DRESSES, 4. MARLIES, 5. RANGER, 6. ROOM, 10. PRAIRIE, 11. MANAGER, 12. SPARKS, 13. SMYTHE, 15. FOUR.

Vancouver Canucks
ACROSS 1. SEDINS, 3. NORRIS, 7. ADIEU, 8. SIXTEEN, 9. SKED, 11. ROSS, 14. RUSSIAN, 16. BOOTH, 17. HENRIK, 18. ROGERS.
DOWN 1. SUNDAY, 2. NASLUND, 4. RANGERS, 5. SECOND, 6. VETS, 10. KASSIAN, 11. ROBERTO, 12. CROUCH, 13. CHECKS, 15. NINE.

Washington Capitals
ACROSS 1. HOLTBY, 3. MOSCOW, 7. EXTRA, 8. MAKES DO, 9. AWAY, 11. WING, 14. CHIMERA, 16. NORTH, 17. SWEDEN, 18. BROOKS.
DOWN 1. HUNTER, 2. BURNABY, 4. CARLSON, 5. WILSON, 6. ADAM, 10. WHISTLE, 11. WINKLER, 12. SCOUTS, 13. SHARKS, 15. ALEX.

Winnipeg Jets
ACROSS 1. ONDREJ, 3. LITTLE, 7. RIFLE, 8. DEFENSE, 9. MANN, 11. EGOS, 14. ALL-STAR, 16. SWEDE, 17. ROARED, 18. SMYTHE.
DOWN 1. OILERS, 2. EASTERN, 4. TORONTO, 5. ELEVEN, 6. LADD, 10. ATLANTA, 11. ENSTROM, 12. CALDER, 13. CENTRE, 15. RICK.

Word Searches

ANAHEIM DUCKS

```
B R E L S E K N A Y R O B
O R E T U S N A Z R S P X
U C B O B M U R R A Y E G
D F K P A C I F I C C H N
R A I S L E F G Q E O I I
E L R S O Y M A H N R O W
A Z O E E S J P D T E R D
U T P A U L K A R I Y A L
B E L Y L R A C I U P T I
L G G Q E M H N Z G E D W
E I R E N O T S N H R Y E
R N E S I J A P H E R Z Y
S T A N L E Y C U P Y D K
```

ARIZONA COYOTES

```
D Q R W I N N I P E G F K
R D I J R R A N O E L S U
S H A N E D O A N R T A H
H O H G K T Y Q N T A N C
T W A R D L S O E A E L A
I L M E E T A P Y L B O K
M E D T O G P R A W M K T
S R S Z B I P T N W J Y V
E O L K T U I H D L E N A
K N U Y T V H C L B C B W
I A N H K C I N E O R U A
M G L E N D A L E K T D N
I H L H N A Q K I S T S S
```

BOSTON BRUINS

```
C S G A R D E N A B O W S
K N I S G G O H I O T H A
M A R C H A N D Z U O M I
E O T I S O P S E Q R D L
C P I R B E A U N U U B E
A Y C S E C N U O E S V R
M Y J Y R R E H C U R R A
N E E Y G S I N H L A N I
E T R S E D L R A S K C H
E B K I R P U Z R S N O C
L Q X K O L J O A N C N P
Y A N E N A X L S S E M Q
```

BUFFALO SABRES

```
S S N I A G A R A C O W F
A N O S G D O H I S T O L
B C I H T O R N E I I M A
R L T Q A O O Z M G M V F
E R C L N E P L Y I M D O
T P E R R E A U L T U B N
O Y N S V C N U O D R V T
O Y N P H L K F F U R L A
T E O Y R S S N O L A N I
H T C S Z E D I O A Y C N
F B V Y D P E Z N S N O E
Y Q X K Q L U O I N C N P
T H E A U D X L S S E M Q
```

CALGARY FLAMES

```
H C F L E T C H E R I G B
G I L A X H U B K P S P E
I E K R U B N A I R B S P
H A R T L E Y G P B A I L
S I E I K E I H Q E G N C
O C L A N N Y X U E I N V
S A D D L E D O M E O I O
N T U A U S D L O A R C D
M L H V A U V Z N L D A E
Z A Z Q Y E V R A H A M U
Y N M H E S R I H N N Y T
R T K A R R I R A M O O Y
I A P U C Y E L N A T S K
```

CAROLINA HURRICANES

```
S Q K H U D O B I N E O B
R E L Y Q G H B K P S B E
U C K R R H G I E L A R A
T R F E D A L C P B A I L
H L L R E J O R D A N C
E A E K O A A F U E I D F
R A Y D F F D R A W M A C
F T B M T S D A J A U M D
O S T V R U V N E L E O E
R C Z Q A O H C K B C U U
D I T H H R T I E N I R T
R R I W P Y T S U L T T Y
I E P U C Y E L N A T S K
```

CHICAGO BLACKHAWKS

```
S H K H U D K B I N E R B
P Q U E N N E V I L L E E
A C K L R H O S W E O T A
T R K E L A T S P B E N L
R G L E N N H A L L S E C
I A E L I A A F U E P C V
C A Y U R T D R A W O D C
K T B P T N H A J A S E S
K W T S T A N M I K I T A
A C D Q A M H C Z B T I V
N D R O F W A R C N O N A
E R I K O O R B A E S U R
I E S J A B R L O K T S D
```

COLORADO AVALANCHE

```
K S T I G I N L A N E D P
Y A D A M F O O T E M E C
D E M L E U R K U M P L S
N N P I R O D L S S A E N
J O E S A K I C I L T T L
S N E H L G Q A Y N R A A
G N Y E S O U H O Q I L N
I I C R E F E N E H C U D
G K X M I R S P D E K O E
U C U A K S O U A W R N S
E A V N C K N Z R S O I K
R M P O O R E I L L Y N O
E A S J R E V N E D K M G
```

COLUMBUS BLUE JACKETS

```
B N S J O R I C K N A S H
Y D T R T L K L E S L A C
V L A L P U R K D D C B S
E I Z K E N A K W A I B Y
J F U I S G V A N H X R K
O G Y T N O N L O C O O S
H N C O S A H A I I R V N
A I X N N E E I T R A S I
N R U A U S T N A W I K B
S P V L D K N E N S H Y U
E S P O U E D N L D E N D
N A T I L O P O R T E M H
```

DALLAS STARS

```
D M A U M U T O L V E O T
H I T C H C O C K R S U E
N K O N J L E P A J R E X
I E S E A K I N Y C O P A
K M E S M N E T O R B L S
H O N S I Y J A U B I E E
S D N E E E L J N R Y H F
U A I A B G I T R O E T E
H N M V E M U S I U N O R
C O G Q N M H I Z G T N S
I I T I N R U T N H I E Y
N L S I R A P H C H N Q
I L I N D Y R U F F W D K
```

DETROIT RED WINGS

```
H H R G R E B R E T T E Z
T J D E L V E C C H I O L
W Y A S D N I L A N N W L
E E T R V K C O C B A B A
L L S A W C H U K B L Y W
I T Y Z U B H Y N D F A N
D V U Z T Z R O F K R M O
S I K A E D R P W S E O R
T S N Z E R M U T E D M K
R U O H O V M S S T S N S
O J R H O L L A N D S P S
M S U P O T C O N C O Z H
Y J O E L O U I S I N A I
```

EDMONTON OILERS

```
R Y A N S M Y T H V E O T
H K T P H S O A K G S U D
N Z Q O J E E Y A R L E X
I T S C F C C L Y A U P A
K E A K I N S O O N E L M
H R N L G E J R F T L E E
A G P I D R L H C F R H F
L A I N B E I A R U E T L
B N M G E F M L I H B Y L
E O G T A U H L Z R E N A
R I T O N P U T N H I E X
T N S N E V I R C S H N E
A L Y N D O M E S S I E R
```

FLORIDA PANTHERS

```
B S S J O C H E A N E D M
Y L T B O L L A N D M A H
D N A L D U R K S M C L S
N A N I O O D L S L I E N
E R L K E N A L E L L T U
N L E S S G T A Y N H A A
I S Y V I O N H O O Q Y L E
K F C O R E A S B T R L D
O E X N N R L P D E W O R
J T U A U S L U A W Z N E
E L V V S K A Z R S H I B
Y F P O U E G L B D E N U
K A S J I W E I S S K M H
```

LOS ANGELES KINGS

```
S S N G R E T Z K Y O W L
A N O S N S O H I S T O A
D C I H T O R S U T T E R
R I T Q A R H Z M G R V O
E R O L N L P C N W O R B
R P E N R E A U A T L B I
A Y Y C N M N U O V Y V T
T Y T J H E S F F U A R A
I E H R R S E L P A T S I
P T G T C A R T E R U C L
O Q U I C K E Z N S N O L
K Q O K Q L U O I N C N E
V A D I D R A B M O L M Q
```

MINNESOTA WILD

```
H Q Z U M U T O L V E O B
P R E T U S N A Y R S P X
O C F E G L E M A I R E C
M D K E F O O L P S A C E
I D I S L E F U Q E H I L
N C R L E Y L A U B I O E
V H O E T E L P N R K R N
I A B A C K S T R O M E E
L R A V H I V S I U R T R
L D G Q E M H V Z G C D G
E I T H R R U T E H I Y Y
R N E S I R A P H C A Z Y
I G C I Y V O S A M P D K
```

MONTRÉAL CANADIENS

```
H Q Z U M U R O F V E O B
G I L A X H U B K P S P E
I C B E R G E V I N K A P
L R F V A A L C P B A C L
S I L I K E F H Q E H I C
O C E L Y O A X U E I O V
H H S E R F L T P K R R O
N A B B U S D L J A N E D
M R T V A U V Z E L E T E
Z D Z Q I H H X Z B C T U
Y T H E R R I E N I Y T
R V I W P X V K P E R O Y
I H C I L V O H A M P D K
```

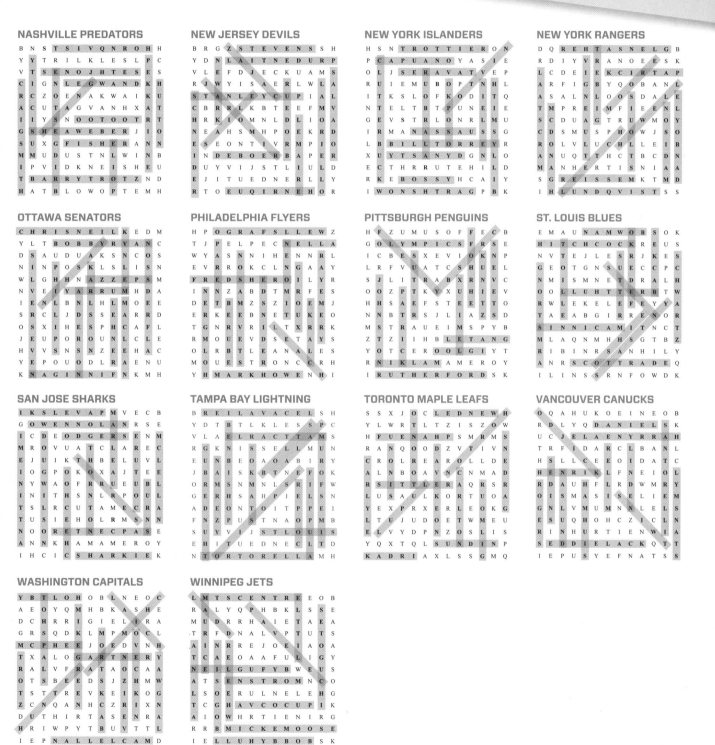

NASHVILLE PREDATORS

```
B N S T S I V Q N R O H H
Y Y T R I L K L E S L P C
V T S E N O J H T E S E S
C I G N L E G W A N D K H
R C Z O E N A K W A I K U
A C U T A G V A N H X A T
I I Y S N O O T O O T R T
G S H E A W E B E R J I O
S U X G F I S H E R A N N
M M U D U S T N L W I N B
I P V I D K N E I S H E U
T B A R R Y T R O T Z N D
H A T B L O W O P T E M H
```

OTTAWA SENATORS

```
C H R I S N E I L K E D M
Y L T B O B B Y R Y A N C
D S A U D U A K S N C O S
N I N P O S K L S L I S N
W L G H H N A Z Z E P S M
N V E I Y A R R U M H D A
I E N L B N L H L M O E E
S R C L J D S S E A R R D
O S X I H E S P H C A F L
J E U P O R O U N L C L E
Y F V S N S N S N Z E E H A C
Y E P O U O D L R A E N U
K N A G I N N I F N K M H
```

SAN JOSE SHARKS

```
I K S L E V A P M V E C B
G O W E N N O L A N R S E
I C D E O D G E R S E N M
M R O V U A T C L A R E C
E J U I K T H B E L U V L
I O G P O K O X A J T E E
N Y W A O F R R U E U B L
I N I T H S N L R P O U L
T S L R C U T A M E C R A
T U S I E H O L R M S N N
N O O R E T N E C P A S E
A N N K H A M A M E R O Y
I H C I C S H A R K I E K
```

WASHINGTON CAPITALS

```
Y B T L O H O B L N E O C
A E O Y Q M H B K A S H E
D C H R R I G I E L I R A
G R S Q D K L M P M O C L
M C P H E E J O E D V N H
T X A L O G A R T N E R Y
R A L V F R A T A O C A A
O T S B E E D S J Z H M W
T S T T R E V K E I K O G
Z C N Q A N H C Z R I X N
D U T H I R T A S E N R A
H R I W P Y T B U V T T L
I E P N A L L E L C A M D
```

NEW JERSEY DEVILS

```
B R G Z S T E V E N S S H
Y D N L A I T N E D U R P
V L E F D J E C K U A M S
R J W Y I S A E R L W L A
S T A N L E Y C U P I A L
C B R R L K B T E E F M V
H R K I O M N L D L I O A
N E A H S M H P O E K R D
E S E O N T I V R M P I O
I N D E B O E R B A P E R
D U Y V I J S T L I U L D
E J I T U E D N E R L L Y
R T O E U Q I R N E H O R
```

PHILADELPHIA FLYERS

```
H P O G R A F S L L E W Z
T J P E L P E C N E L L A
W Y A S N N I H E N N R L
E V R R O K C L N G A A Y
F R E D S H E R O I L Y R
I N N Z A B D T M R F E S
D E T B M Z S Z I O E M J
E R K E E B N E T U K E O
T G N R V R I L T X R R K
R M O U E V D S E T A Y S
O L R B T L E A N A L E S
M O U E S T R O N C C R H
Y H M A R K H O W E N H I
```

TAMPA BAY LIGHTNING

```
B R E I L A V A C E L S H
Y D T B T L K L E S S P C
V L A E L R A C T T A M S
R G K N I S S E L L M U N
E U N B E O A O A B I R Y
J B A I S K B T N E F O K
O R M S N M N L S R I F W
G E R H S A H P I E L S N
A D E O N T O I T P P E I
F N Z P U S T N A O P M B
S U Y V I J S T L O U I S
E H I T U E D N E C L T D
N T O R T O R E L L A M H
```

WINNIPEG JETS

```
L M T S C E N T R E E O B
R A L Y Q P H B K L S S E
M U D R R H A I E T A E A
T R F D N A L V P T U T S
A I N R R E J O E I A O A
T C A E O A A F U L I G Y
N E I L G U F Y B W E U S
A T S E N S T R O M N C O
L S O E R U L N E L E H G
T C G H A V C O C U P I K
A I O W H R T I E N I R G
R R B M I C K E M O O S E
I E L L U H Y B B O B S K
```

NEW YORK ISLANDERS

```
H S N T R O T T I E R O N
P C A P U A N O Y A S I E
O L J S E R A V A T V E P
R U I E M U B O P T N H L
I T K S L O F K O D I T Q
N T E L T B T P U N E I E
G E V S T R L O N R L M U
I R M A N A S S A U S S G
L B B I L L T O R R E Y R
X U Y T S A N Y D G N L O
E C T H R R U T E H I L D
R K E B O S S Y H C A I Y
I W O N S H T R A G P B K
```

PITTSBURGH PENGUINS

```
H F Z U M U S O F F E C B
G O L Y M P I C S F R S E
I C B E S X E V I O K N P
L R F V U A T C S H U E L
S J L I T R A B X R N V C
O O Z P T K Y X U H I E V
H H S A E F S T E E T T O
N N B T R S J L I A Z S D
M S T R A U E I M S P Y B
Z T Z I I H B L E T A N G
Y O T C E R O O L G I Y T
R N I K L A M A M E R O Y
I R U T H E R F O R D S K
```

TORONTO MAPLE LEAFS

```
S S X J O C L E D N E W H
Y L W R T L T Z I S Z O W
H F U E N A H P S M R M S
R A N Q O O D Z V T I V N
C R O L R E A R O L L D E
A L N B O A V N C N M A D
R S I T T L E R A Q R S R
L U S A U L K O R T U O A
Y E X P R X E R L E O K G
L T U J U D O E T W M E U
E L V Y D P N Z O S L I S
Y Q X T Q L S U N D I N P
K A D R I A X L S S G M Q
```

NEW YORK RANGERS

```
D Q R E H T A S N E L G B
R D I Y V R A N O E E S K
L C D E I E K C I R T A P
A R F I G B Y Q O B A N L
A S A L N L O O S D A L E
T M P R E I M F I E E N L
S C D U A G T R U W M O Y
C D S M U S P H O W J S O
R O L V L U C H L L E I B
A N U Q T T H C T B C D N
M A N H E R T I S N I A A
S G R E I S S E M K T M D
I H L U N D Q V I S T S S
```

ST. LOUIS BLUES

```
E M A U N A M W O B S O K
H I T C H C O C K R E U S
N V T E J L E S R J K E S
G E O T G N S U E C C P C
N M I S M N E T D R A L H
O O L L U H T T E R B T W
R W L E K E L E F E Y A
T A E A B G I R R E N O R
S I N N I C A M I T N C T
M L A Q N M H H S G T B Z
R I B I N R S A N H I L Y
A N R S C O T T R A D E Q
I L I N S S R N F O W D K
```

VANCOUVER CANUCKS

```
O Q A H U K O E I N E O B
R D L Y Q D A N I E L S K
U C J E L A E N Y R R A H
T R F I D A R C L B A N L
H S L L C E E O I D A T C
H E N R I K L F N E I O I
R D A U H F L R D W M R Y
O I S M A S I S E L I E M
G N L V M U M N N L E L S
E S U Q H O H C Z I C L N
R I N H U R T I E N W I A
S E D D I E L A C K Q T T
I E P U S Y E F N A T S S
```

ACKNOWLEDGMENTS

ONLY ONE PERSON HAS HIS NAME SLAPPED ON THE COVER, but all the credit goes to those he's indebited to for helping to take *The Big Book of Hockey Fun* all the way from idea to print:

Jason Kay, The Hockey News' editor in chief, for entrusting me with all the responsibilities.

Edward Fraser, THN's managing editor, for his empathy and humor.

Jacqueline Loch, THN's publisher, and Marc Laberge, book publisher, for their work behind the scenes.

Susan Antonacci, associate publisher, for her swiftness, sleight of hand and staunch support in dealing with all the dirty details that bedevil the book process.

THN staffers Ken Campbell, Ryan Kennedy, Matt Larkin and Adam Proteau, for lending their slick storytelling chops.

Freelancers Eric Stephens, Mike Loftus, John Vogl, Randy Sportak, Adrian Dater, Aaron Portzline, Mike Heika, Bob Duff, George Richards, Doug Ward, Michael Russo, Ryan Dixon, David Boclair, Rich Chere, Steve Zipay, Murray Pam, Wayne Fish, Sarah McLellan, Shelly Anderson, David Pollak, Jeremy Rutherford, Ben Kuzma, Brian McNally and Tim Campbell, for their expertise and coverage.

Puzzle maker Larry Humber and illustrator Robert Ullman, for their playful contributions.

Luke Sawczak, for his perfectionist proofreading.

Intrepid interns Ashley Casey, Gustan Koumantaros, Michael Musalem, Ainsley Smith and Ari Yanover, for sweating the small stuff in the final stages.

Casey Ippolito, for his fearless fact-checking.

Josh Elliott, for filling in a few holes.

Erin Quinn, Carlie McGhee and Alyson Young, THN's marketing/communications representatives, for getting the word out across the hockey world.

And especially Erika Vanderveer, the book's all-star art director, for her dynamic design and endless revisions.

– RONNIE SHUKER